"A laugh on every page, Christina   e

western world."

–Robert F. Kennedy Jr.

"Oxenberg's musings on local culture suggests a style that hints of Tom Wolfe,
but with the detached wry and dry observation of Joan Didion, tossed with more
than a splash of charming, classy, self-deprecating amusing neurotica that is all
her own."

–Dale Launer *My Cousin Vinny*, *Dirty Rotten Scoundrels*

"Christina Oxenberg is not only the hottest but also the edgiest writer to emerge
this year. Don't miss the thrill of reading her new book."

–Edward J. Epstein *The Hollywood Economist: The Hidden Financial Reality*
Behind the Movies

"Oxenberg has always scandalized polite society—she is, after all, the daughter
of a royal princess—and has chosen to live in the manner of her writing:
outrageously, ironically, comically at times, but fearlessly brave and above all
true and fresh."

–Taki

"Cynics will want to knock it, considering the pedigree it comes from, but that will be tough because Royal Blue's version of a bad and privileged childhood is funny, fetching, and full of gorgeous writing with a deep, tugging undercurrent of melancholy. Its intimate rendering of wealth without cliché is a triumph —imagine Evelyn Waugh rewriting Elöise. For a first novel, what's most remarkable is that there's not a bum sentence in the entire thing."

–Bret Easton Ellis *American Psycho*

"Oxenberg depicts in exquisite detail the grotesque side of privilege."

–Dominick Dunne *A Season in Purgatory*

"This book will curl your hair, with humor, tragedy and modern despair."

–Eve Babitz *Black Swans*

"This story is full of zest and humor, but the pain borne by the increasingly streetwise heroine permeates every page. I think the book is excellent: very compelling and very well written."

–Hugo Vickers *Cecil Beaton: A Biography*

"Darkly funny."

–CHICAGO TRIBUNE

"Oxenberg shows herself a master at pulling away comfortable, familiar ground... Oxenberg creates a languid, ferociously beautiful and barbarous world, with an atmosphere reminiscent of that which pervades the work of F. Scott Fitzgerald..."

–THE INDEPENDENT NEWSPAPER, UK

"Though Oxenberg insists the book 'is not a tell-all,' its portrait of a daughter and her charmingly irresponsible European princess mother echoes Christina's relationship with Elizabeth, a socialite who counts Prince Charles as her second cousin..."

–PEOPLE MAGAZINE

Christina Oxenberg (signature)

Christina Oxenberg

Do These Gloves

Make My Ass Look Fat?

Acknowledgement is made to the following, in which various forms of this

book's pieces first appeared: "A Final Fling" first appeared in *Penthouse* © 2001

by General Media Communications, Inc. All rights reserved. Used by special

permission of General Media Communications, Inc., a subsidiary of FriendFinder

Networks Inc. "My Date with Steve" in *Allure* © 1998, "Kind Hearts and

Coronets" in *The London Sunday Times Magazine* © 1997, "Stars and Bars" in

Tatler © 1996, various articles in *Takimag.com* © 2009.

Table of Contents

Also by Christina Oxenberg

Royal Blue

And

TAXI

Foreword

THE FRAGILE BOUNDARIES between elation and mania, and between a crazy person and a highly sensitive one, are, as to be expected, extremely fine. Christina Oxenberg's articles have always fascinated me because of their manic sensitivity, but above all, her ability to write about her true feelings without sounding trite or corny. Letting it all hang out is a Sixties trait that is boring, phony and trite. She manages to let it all hang out and it sounds fresh and true. She acts out her fantasies but her hold on reality never diminishes. She abjures that frightful bore that's ritual marriage and those glittering balls that go with it. Oxenberg has always scandalized polite society—she is, after all, the daughter of a royal princess—and has chosen to live in the manner of her writing: outrageously, ironically, comically at times, but fearlessly brave and above all true and fresh.

Taki

A very special thank you to *Taki*

Do These Gloves

Make My Ass Look Fat?

My Date with Steve Martin

I GO TO THIS SWANKY BEVERLY HILLS PARTY and there is Steve Martin. An actor who I have never particularly cared for. Anyway, to my surprise he appears to be paying attention to me. Every time I glance up, he is looking directly at me. This is the oddest thing, but it has happened once before, with a famous tennis player, so it is not entirely outlandish, I assure myself. At one point he sidles past me while I speak to someone. He moves by me very slowly; I do not look at him but can feel his eyes are glued to me.

Later, I am on the phone with Matilda, and she tells me she knows this guys who sells Steve paintings. She'll check this out. She calls me back with excellent news: Steve likes English-accented, mousy, brainy brunets; I'm his type. Later still she tells me he is shy, that he never approaches girls. He was looking at me. He definitely was looking at me.

Matilda says she is going to get me Steve for a husband, that we're perfect for each other, and that she knows exactly how to pull this off. I say, "OK, but go slowly and keep me posted all the way. I have the power to veto any of your choices." She agrees. But she is a major con artist, so why do I believe her? I guess it suits me.

Time flies. I'm busy writing my novel, and even though I've told all my close friends that I think Steve Martin was looking at me at this party that I went to, it all gradually fades into the background.

Then one morning the phone rings; it's Matilda. She tells me that she called Steve's doorman and left Steve a message from me. I know she is kidding, and I am too cool to appear shocked by anything, so I laugh and say, "that would be funny."

And she says, "You wouldn't be mad at me?"

And I reply, "No, I would think it was funny, but don't, whatever you do, don't do it."

An hour later the phone rings again. It's a gentleman claiming to be Steve Martin. I am impressed with the lengths Matilda is willing to go for a laugh. "Ha, ha," I trilled at the prankster. "How nice for you."

18

"Sometimes it is," he says.

Wow, I think, this guy is good, but I am not about to falter and fall for the gag. "It was great to see you at the party," "Steve" is saying as I pace about with the telephone jammed against my head, trying my best to line the voice up with his voice. It sounds eerily similar. "I was so pleased to get your message," he says. "Really, I didn't think you would call me."

"Who am I speaking with?" I demand.

"Steve Martin." He says softly, "how is your book coming along?"

"What?" I say, sighing, as I stare at myself in a mirror, making faces of incredulity. All right, I think, if you're going to keep up this charade, so am I.

"She told you about my book?" I add somewhat under my breath. "How much did she pay you for this?"

"Can we have lunch one day soon?"

"Lunch?" I think for certain that at this point he will confess to the hoax. Instead, he asks me more questions about my immediate life: where I live, how long I've been here. He laughs after my every sarcasm. Furthermore, he sounds giddy, in love. Before I hang up, I agree to lunch.

I speed-dial Matilda and interrogate her. "I told you I can do anything," She cajoles, assuring me it was him. "What happens next is up to you."

Hoping against hope that for once in my life something truly phenomenal is occurring, I have to take this a bit seriously. First thing is to rent all his movies, including his directorial efforts. I study. I revise my earlier distaste. I realize my future husband is exceptionally talented. Second, I make an appointment at the dentist, to get my teeth cleaned.

Sunday morning the same male voice is again on my telephone. After my back-to-back viewing of his entire oeuvre, I know the voice. The ramifications are mesmerizing, colossal. It's a funny thing, I think, usually I attract psychos.

I arrive early at the restaurant. I have a newspaper as a prop but keep one eyeball on the front door. Five minutes later Steve Martin, in person, in a slack hat and soft layers, stands at the door, looking about the mostly empty restaurant. I am extremely composed, waiting for him to throw himself down on bended knee and ask me to marry him. He looks at me, and then again at the empty room, and then back at me. He frowns. "Are you Christina?" he asks, peering at me.

"Yes." I say, and add half-jokingly, "is something wrong?" I sit up straight, and wait for him to swoon under the influence of love. Instead, he says, "You don't look anything like how I remember you." He looks sincerely perplexed.

Ignoring the sour turn, I go ahead with my prepared speech which is to assure him that it was not I who left the message with his doorman. "How do you mean?" he demands, dead serious, looming over the table. "Who did then? What's going on?"

I had thought we would laugh it off as one of Cupid's many funny ways. His fury catches me quite off guard. "I'm the subject of a prank?" he spits out, shoving his hands deep down to the bottom of his coat pockets. I expect him to turn and leave, but since he does not I am obliged to offer some sort of explanation. I decide to lie, vigorously. I turn it all around and blame the bungle on him.

"After all," I point out, my voice trembling, "you knew my name, you called me. I never even believed it was you on the phone. Who did you think I was?"

"Who did you think you were meeting here?" he asks, still standing behind a chair, fingering the rim of it.

"I hadn't a clue," I tell him, truthfully.

Inexplicably, he sits down. Apparently there was another Christina with an English accent, whom he had run into at some party, who was also writing a book. He had asked her to call him, and he had supposed that he was meeting her for lunch.

"This is enormously embarrassing," I babble, on automatic. "Really unforgivable..." I maunder on seemingly for hours, masterfully divvying up the blame between himself and Matilda, who, under the circumstances will have to forgive me this treason. At no point do I mention any abstract plans of marriage.

"Who is Matilda?"

"A friend," I offer, careful not to taint myself with conspiracy. "She's a funny girl. Really, if you met her, you'd probably like her. For one thing she is unusually beautiful…"

A waiter comes by with menus. His simple suggestion of an aperitif seems surreal.

"She sounds psychotic," Mr. Martin says, never looking up from his menu, and then orders himself a salad and a plate of pasta.

"I'll have the same," I finally manage, pointing surreptitiously at Mr. Martin with my chin.

Mr. Martin says, "Tell me about yourself," and shoves his chair back a few feet, crossing his legs. He does not crack a smile.

Moments pass and most of a paper napkin disintegrates in my nervous hands. I think I might have a heart attack. Meanwhile I recognize the benefits of surviving such an ordeal. I know people who pay big money to experience terror, as a character enhancer.

I fold my hands in my lap and take a deep breath. "I'm not a Brit," I begin, by way of explanation, "but I grew up in England, hence the accent. It's a fake, or rather, I'm a fraud." His face remains impassive. Staring at the whiteness of the tablecloth, I continue, breathing deeply between sentences for fortification. One miserable anecdote at a time, I claw my way up the cliff face of this disaster. I chat on while he eats pasta, spinning tines in the oily strands. If I did not know better I would suppose he is relaxing. But I had heard him on the telephone when he thought I was someone he liked. At no point during the meal does he sound like that man.

He orders coffee after lunch, a sure sign of peace, but I decline a cup myself, fearing it would launch my already taut nerves into the stratosphere.

It is a relief to watch him walk away. I back into a deli and buy myself a pack of cigarettes. I smoke them all the way down to stubs in less than an hour as I tramp homeward, more vividly awake than I have ever been in my life.

The episode was so embarrassing I actually thought it might have bonded us for all time. I thought it might be a second beginning, now that I'd proved myself. But it wasn't even a first. I never heard from him again.

Royal Blues

ACCORDING TO THE CHINESE, as of February 8 this year we entered the Year of the Ox. On that night, I went to Chinatown to celebrate with won ton and green tea and to light sticks of incense and anything else that I thought might help dispel the noxious curse that surrounds me. I am not generally endowed with luck, so in a bid to improve matters, I had latched onto the remote but possible connection between thousands of years of mysticism and the first syllable of my last name.

But by mid-April, three months before my novel, *Royal Blue*, a coming-of-age tale about a girl with royal connections—pure coincidence, of course

—was due to be published, instead of raucous success I could only see the abyss of silence yawning. My publicist at Simon & Schuster called to tell me she was leaving at the end of the week. Someone new would be tending to me. Suddenly, I saw how easy it would be to be forgotten. Perhaps this Year of the Ox thing was only for a chosen few.

Panicky, I sought advice, only to amass a ton of contradictory suggestions. Some told me to hire a public-relations firm, others told me not to because it would cheese off my publisher's press department. I speed-dialed my editor, Bob.

Bob is the grand old wizard who found me three years ago and gave me a contract. Two things, he told me, sell a book: word of mouth and luck. Compile a list of influential people, he advised, a "big mouth list." Aware of my strained relationship with my family he also recommended I include my mother Princess Elizabeth of Yugoslavia, my father and sister and their closest friends. "It's time to be shameless, Ox." He coached, "this is business."

Trembling, I opened my address book and set about mailing 250 books with groveling letters, including a cutting from a local gossip column referring to the tantalizing rumor that my father may or may not have been President John Fitzgerald Kennedy.

"Ignore the critics and don't read the reviews: your goal is a pound of press," advised Bob. I installed a small weighing machine on my desk, and everyday balanced whatever coverage I had managed to gather on top of it. In two weeks I had a quarter pound.

Friends fanned out, exploiting their particular areas of expertise, spoon-feeding the media, arranging subsidized book parties at ritzy restaurants, standing-room-only readings and signings at bookshops, and even a fully underwritten fete in a sumptuous baroque spread at the Dakota, where gloved waiters served blue drinks in martini glasses and Larry Rivers and his Climax Band played the "royal" blues.

Meanwhile my mailbox began to fill up with missives. Elizabeth Taylor penned on powder-blue stationery: "We will surely enjoy reading this volume." (Long considered Hollywood royalty Ms. Taylor can forgivably refer to herself as "we.")

Prince and Princess Michael of Kent wrote on royal-blue stationery (matching envelope with elegant white lettering, a tall "M" under a crown): "The title is certainly uncompromising," and that they planned to "explore it with care."

My mother's brother, Prince Alexander of Yugoslavia wrote (white card, grey embossed Serbian crown) to thank me for "sending this very explosive book, most amusing and so true."

Even my accountant wrote, on red paper with matching envelope—very bad taste, I thought. It appeared that the long-awaited "buzz" had finally begun.

I have heard that my mother calls me a "Menendez child" (remember those parent-killing tennis boys?) for having written *Royal Blue*, which, although a work of fiction, some claim has elements of the *roman à clef* about it. On the other hand, I have also heard that she has yet to read it.

Whatever the case, the good news is that her cries of victimization are positive signs that Bob is a brilliant strategist.

The bad news, however, is that no British publishing house will take up my novel. It seems nobody dares. What with British libel laws and the clear and present danger of my mother and her strident plans to sue, there's little incentive. The marketing plans, it seems, are almost working *too* well, terrorizing the timorous.

One month after the book was officially born, I had accumulated a little under a half pound of coverage. Then came the *coup de grace*, the cover of *New York* magazine. For the photo session I wore my smartest suit, a brand new black Calvin Klein affair bought for me by an admiring aunt. "Unless the Pope gets shot, you're on the cover," they told me on the day of the session. Unfortunately, so excited was I by this news that I backed into a wall of fresh, sticky, glossy white paint, which stained my left buttock with a full moon of whiteness. I decided against demanding that the dry-cleaning bill be paid and took the subway home in order to change and deliver my wrecked garb to the cleaners.

"There's no way this paint will come out, no way," I was told, but I asked them to try anyway, sighing with resignation. The suit, after all, was a small price to pay in lieu of the sales of my book.

Two days after *New York* magazine came out, Gianni Versace was shot dead outside his Miami home. Clutched in the designer's hands as he fell to the ground were *People*, *Vogue* and *New York*—the latter, of course with me on the front. I sighed with relief, realizing that had this tragedy occurred only a few days before, I would have been bumped from the cover and relocated to some quiet page within.

No disrespect, Mr. Versace, but things do seem to be changing for the better. Simon & Schuster's publicity department is an orchestra of phones ringing on my behalf. The cleaners presented me with my suit, all traces of paint removed.

"Very lucky, missy," they told me, "very lucky." For the first time I thought myself blessed, freshly anointed with celestial good fortune, an end at last to the years of bad joss.

Until later, stomping around at home with a bowl full of cornflakes, when I tripped over a fan, I slid and lurched and the contents of my cereal bowl lunged at the fast spinning blades. Cornflakes applied themselves to far walls, milk dripped eerily over my plastic-wrapped Calvin Klein suit. Cereal murder. Sorry, Mr. Versace, bad taste, I know. But this is business.

Devil Dogs

THE PARTY WAS OVER. We stood at the top of the stairs, and when the front door slammed a welcome sense of peace plummeted. Now it was just me and my guy John, his son Tad and Tad's girl, Esme. That moment of calm was shattered when John began animatedly chatting up Esme. John's efforts were dubious at best seeing as Esme was coma-drunk and only standing by a miracle.

Tad was a decade my junior, while John had a score on me. I met Tad for the first time that night but I wasn't surprised to find him sexy, and outrageous, rather like his father. Tad and I leaned against a marble column, our faces inches apart, silently watching Esme staring sweetly if unconsciously up at John. As I was mentally calculating how far John might take this opportunity, given the chance, Tad lowered his head to my neck and gave me a languid kiss. It startled me, and I spluttered nervous giggles, but I made no effort to scuttle out of reach. Decorum, I decided, was already moot, given the scenario.

Tad did not stop. I saw John notice, he did a speedy double take, and then he pretended he hadn't. Tad was nuzzling with tiny kisses inching slowly around my neck. John prattled all the more intently at fragile Esme. The girl was delicate as a blade of grass, and she swayed in the breeze of John's blather.

Tad's kisses were tender, unhurried, confident. I did nothing to stop him; I'll admit I may have leaned in a fraction. His kisses were warm. Hot, in fact, hot as hell. Hell being where I was surely destined.

"Tad?" John at last exploded, laughing perhaps just a little too exuberantly. John marched toward me, took me by the hand, led me away. I followed without looking back. Our private party had just begun.

I saw his son's face in his; saw how their lips were identical.

I Scream

IN DEFERENCE TO THE TRADITION of presenting a gift to one's host I gave

serious consideration to what, exactly, I should bring when I was invited to lunch

this past Sunday. I cruised the aisles of a local fancy foods establishment and

dawdled a long while in front of a freezer packed with ice creams. I salivated at

the descriptions of just about everything. But no, I thought, it didn't seem quite

right. Vaguely, I surmised, ice cream was better suited to a tragic lonely

afternoon. I settled on a bouquet of wild flowers.

Because this is the Hamptons (and despite the fact the colorful fronds

were probably ripped from the delicatessen's back yard) they cost near eight thousand dollars, and I'm only exaggerating the littlest bit. My appetite was struck a blow by this gouge: nevertheless, onward I went to the house of my host.

Said host took the florid bunch from me and, with a pair of kitchen scissors, he snipped off the cellophane wrapping. Then, in an imperceptible millisecond his tiny daughter's fingertip met with the scissor blades. No one knows exactly how this happened but the little girl broke out in squeals of pain as blood gushed over a plate of uncooked prawns. The tip of her finger hung loose.

Good dad that he is, he bustled the sobbing child into his SUV and made off for the hospital for a stitch or two to repair the finger. Later I would learn the damage was permanent.

And then all was quiet in the magnificent, ultra-modern beach house. Left behind with the as yet uncooked comestibles, aubergines, filet mignon, the aforementioned pale grey prawns which still dripped with dollops of blood, I was in no mood to cook. A quick rummage in the freezer revealed a bounty of frozen desserts. I removed a tub of white chocolate and macadamia nut gelato and repaired to a sun chair. With each spoonful I toasted the otherwise perfect bloody Sunday.

Riders on the Storm

'TIS A WEEKEND in late August and two non-indigenous tribes have descended on the twin forks.

The Hampton Classic Horse Show attracts a crowd of aficionados. For the weeklong event a field is converted into a micro-village. The show is a striking affair. The owners of the fabled beachfront properties are in attendance. The crowd is sleek. Men wear linen, women mostly in white. One super-hottie sucked up all sorts of attention in metallic silver shorts that barely cleared her faultless bottom, high chunky heels, and a tiny, floaty, black thing for a top that mostly worked to advertise the product beneath. The summer sun is hot like a sauna. A leaden humidity is infused with ladies' perfumes and wisps of horse manure.

Riders in tan jodhpurs and spit-polished knee-high leather boots cling in clusters, evoking Degas' dancers. Horses and riders alike are daunting in their perfection. The equestrian world is an art form of its own. Only diehard PETA-heads could fail to note the magnificence.

Meanwhile, a hurricane sent pre-storm threats by manner of line-backer-sized chunky waves. Local surfers pride themselves on tackling the beast at their shores. But a hurricane will draw surfers from long distances, like firemen to a blaze. After a hard day of paddling and defying imminent death the water-babies were to be found at the Stephen Talkhouse nightclub in Amagansett. It was a time to decompress and trade fish tales.

"Only problem was my board hit me in the head, like, 20 times."

"I died twice today. For real! I drowned twice."

An energetic fiesta engaged on the dance floor, a veritable sweat-swamp. The band was bangin'.

Off to one side, in a private world, a couple sat on a bench. Young, supple, luscious, they were making out. She was sitting on his lap and they were kissing. Oblivious. These were the spoils of the day.

A pink-faced Atlanta cherub exclaimed: "I came out here for the weekend and I'm gonna learn how to surf." And then he fell over, crashing into a table of drinks, taking it all down to the sticky dirty floor with him.

Jocko, banker by day and one of the more expert surfers around, was disappointed with the hurricane. "The waves are up to 20 feet, but they're choppy. Not good." With his plastic cup of beer he pointed at Pocahontas Surfer Babe, a tanned, taut, loose-limbed lass, appetizing as a pastry. "I don't care," he said, "because tonight I've fallen in love. I think."

As inevitably as the weekend would end, the hurricane diffused and the storm riders dispersed. Rusted jalopies with surf boards lashed to roofs cruised out of town alongside the very latest in motoring excess. To each his own experience, though never the twain shall meet.

Ess & Em

MY CONDUIT TO THE WORLD of, uh, exotic sex, was to be a fairly disgusting friend of mine. I say disgusting on account of his determination to disrobe me. And I say friend very loosely.

It had been a while but I tracked down Marko. I explained I hoped next time he was in New York City, he would take me with him, when he's next hunting for his octane-sex-fix. I propose a night out at the pleasure and expense of the publication I was working with.

"I'll take you anywhere you want to go." Marko said. "I'll take your clothes off everywhere we go. Heh." I was mildly sickened at the thought.

Months later the day arrived when Marko did, indeed, make it to town. Gradually we shaped a plan around his eating schedule. We'd meet in the middle of the afternoon at a noodle shop near 4th Avenue and 10th Street. From there we would proceed to the W hotel, sip on drinks, and fiddle on the internet. We'd look up Marko's swingers' club websites. He went so far as to entrust me with his secret code to enter the site, in case, "I liked anything I saw." It was going to be a long-ass day. My commitment to the task of investigating the seamy side of life flagged.

As the hour of our appointment drew near Marko left a spray of messages. Each one rawer, dirtier than the last. He somehow managed to inject a visible leer into his tone. Chilling.

Almost too late I saw the imploding obstacle to an evening with a "domi-mondaine." While Marko was an authentic gateway opportunity he was also too authentic, too awful, to be around.

The time for us to meet came and passed and I never picked up the phone or returned messages of any kind from Marko. He went bananas. Left hundreds of entreaties for days on end, right up until the moment he departed, headed whence he sprung.

His pleas were a rainbow of emotions. I was unmoved. I think, for an Ess, he ought to have grudgingly appreciated being "Emmed."

A Pisser

RUMOR HAS IT A LOCAL HAMPTONS restaurant owner has a proclivity

unbecoming to the Michelin-worthy eatery over which he presides. Perhaps

you're familiar with tiny town's gossip du jour? Story is that of an unfortunate

girl named, improbably, Leak. With a name like that she must be progeny from

artsy-diehard tree-hugging types. Little Leak was having none of it. She wanted

the good life. And she had a plan.

On her 18th birthday Leak moved away from her family's hemp

enterprise in the Yakima flats of Washington State. She Greyhounded directly to

the Hamptons, the internationally known enclave of mega-money. A veritable job

fair for pretty girls. Leak has those hillbilly good looks with a mane of hair, and endless legs in cowboy boots, and an awesome rump in white shark-skin shorty-shorts. She knew what her wampum was worth and she planned on getting equal or better on her trade. This gold digger was shovel-ready.

She quickly met a man. On paper he would do. He was wealthy, respected in his milieu, a local notable. Projecting wildly she envisaged her name next to his under their photograph on the society pages. In the flesh he was something to be reckoned with. This man, naked, was doughy. Hindsight was not pretty. He was both thick and spindly, a mélange of loose skin and rough patches; tattoos of his life's map.

Leak's new guy was frequently rude to her, called her an imbecile, a cretin. He insulted her regularly. She took his credit card and shopped. She was blissfully happy. That is until one night in the kitchen of his restaurant.

The kitchen was their "special" place. So this one night, as they were giving in to their urges, Leak hitched herself onto the butcher's block. He advanced on her, unbuckling his belt, his pants tumbled, rumpling to his loafers. He was locked and loaded. She leaned her head back and closed her eyes.

But things were not right. She allowed herself a peek. And in a flash her fairy tale melted forever away. He was indulging himself in the mother of all pisses, washing her down like she was a Humvee in from desert patrol. At least, that is as much as I've heard so far. Will keep you posted if I find out Leak soup is on the menu.

Asshole Tax

WARNING! RICH ASSHOLES are secretly over charged when they behave badly in the ritzy town of Aspen, Colorado if they upset the locals. For a couple of weeks mid-winter and again mid-summer Aspen overflows with visitors who come to play on the slopes and in the rivers. Maybe they stay in one of the high-priced hotels or perhaps own a home of their own, mansions that lie fallow for most of every year. Little Aspen airport is rumored to host the largest fleet of privately owned flying machines when the rich come to town. The rich are easy to spot in their shiny cars and huge fur coats. Men sport costly watches and dyed hair, women's hands hang heavy with diamonds the size of buffalos. Most of these people are perfectly well behaved innocent tourists.

Also occupying the Victorian mining town are the locals. Whether they were reared there or whether they relocated from lesser geographic locations, they tend to have one thing in common, that being they work for a living. They are in the service industry, and they serve the rich.

Twice a year the two groups collide, each dependent on the other for their well being and yet the gulf between them is bridged only by tips and phony smiles. The Aspen service industry is easily mistaken for a servile population because they wear the costumes of servants: hairdressers, fishing guides, shop girls and cashiers. Unlike the "devoted" servant of old, this group exacts revenge regularly when crossed. It is a common, though quiet, practice to charge their customers something known locally as the "asshole tax."

Everyone already knows better than to offend a chef or kitchen staff. George Orwell covered this in detail in "Down and Out in Paris and London." Stories of adulterated food are well documented. But have you heard the rumors in Aspen?

For example: Jake, a hair stylist, says, "most of my customers are cool, but now and then I get a windbag who makes me want to stab her with my scissors. If they are out-of-towners and I know I'm not going to see them again I might leave the bleach on a little too long. Then their hair will break off when they get home. Usually I just charge them a little extra. Could be as little as fifty bucks, but I have been inspired to add $100, even $150." Infractions range from

44

serial rescheduling, being late, tipping badly or aggravating him with showy displays, "why does she have to tell me about her five homes?" Jake complains, "does making me feel like my life is worthless make her feel like a success?"

Dean, a fishing guide, says that he gets along well with most everyone, but now and again he'll be hired by someone "obnoxious," someone who "needs several slices of humble pie." But Dean cannot overtly risk his job so he resorts to sabotage and might not stick worms onto the hooks of his clients fishing poles, or he might steer them towards areas of the river famously fish-free.

Some establishments hang clear signs near their checkout counters asking patrons not to use cell phones when paying. Why? Because, says Becca, "It's friggin' rude." Should a shopper ignore the request and yip and bark into their device, the asshole tax is applied. This tax does not show up on a bill or invoice but is instead stealthily slid into the total. At no point will the customer be clued in to the idea that his/her bad behavior is being anything but worshipped. You have been warned!

Dawned On

5 AM. IT IS STILL NIGHT outdoors, but I hear the early birds whistling. I could wrestle with the bedding some more, or I could give in, get up, and go out. No contest. I clattered out the gravel driveway and directed my car into the dark street. Shadows were smudged by the cast-off from a single street lamp and the traffic lights burning softly at the intersection.

I paused beneath the glowing red man-made star hanging by its cables, the fixture bobbed mildly in place. I waited in the stillness for the red to flood to amber and then to green. And I slid forward, toward nowhere in particular. Out of the gloam came a three quarter ton pickup truck barreling at me, a flashing light pulsing from his dashboard. What?

Next came a minivan, also flaring dashboard bubble lights. I heard no sounds, no sirens. And above the noise of my car's engine I only heard the birds. I rumbled along a flat, windy road heading south to the ocean. The road cuts through a forest thickly populated with short hardy trees shoving their way up and out of a sandy earth. I passed mansions with one, maybe two, lamps lit. The sky was changing from coal to cobalt. I parked at the beach. My footsteps fell deeply into the pliant sand making it slow going from the dunes to the shore.

I scouted for fancy jetsam. I found a clear plastic wine goblet missing its base, the label from a bottle of water, a clump of cocktail napkins and two magazines. I stopped moving and listened to the water licking its way back into the currents, sucking itself back out to sea. Such a tease.

5:30 a.m. the sky is opalescent, with pinks and blues mingling and I head homeward. I avoided hitting a deer, by inches. I was busy congratulating my good luck when I saw a low squat box zoom into the road ahead of me. It is a Mini Cooper. It is navy blue. It hurtled in reverse down a dirt driveway, and spilled into my path.

I know this car. At least, I know the owner. And I had to wonder where was he coming from? Where was he headed? Had he seen me? And, oh, he dates that sexy physical therapist. But she doesn't live anywhere near here, right? Oh, right, got it!

48

As I puzzled the ramifications the Mini pulled ahead, seeming to flatten itself forward into the macadam. The driver appeared to be trying to get away. I wanted to be absolutely sure this was who I thought it was. I applied some pressure to my accelerator. I caught sight of his hat. He never goes anywhere without that straw cowboy hat. The little car surged and darted down a side street, in the direction of the driver's home. Yup, it's that artist dude. He had nothing to fear from me. I was not going be the one to pass along the news of his infidelities. To my thinking there's no need to interfere with nature, especially human nature. Besides, it was just a matter of time, because there are no secrets in tiny town.

It's 6:00 a.m. and I'm home and back in my bed. The birds are booming. I hear the neighbor yelling at his dog to "go lay down." And now I feel I'm ready for sleep.

True Crime

WHY IS THE USA SO FAR DOWN the list in worldwide literacy? How is it that the richest, most advanced country on planet earth lags behind Tajikistan, Tonga and Latvia? (#1 is the Holy See.)

Could it have something to do with the difficulties of becoming a member of a library? Recently when I moved into a rental house I opted not to install cable TV, hoping I could curtail my addiction to reality shows (hideous to admit, yet true, my favorites are the re-enactments of true crime detective stories. I'm prone to watching any crap, the crappier the better). On the calendar it was mid-winter, meanwhile daily the weather fluctuated from below zero to 40 plus. Just this past weekend was all sunshine and cerulean skies. I tromped and skidded atop snow-packed sidewalks to the local library. I made sure to bring some bills in my name to prove I was a candidate for membership.

The library is a towering mass of stone on Main Street just slightly south of the center of town. It sits sedately surrounded by antique residential homes faithful to the styles of Federal and Victorian architecture. Wide steps with handrails lead up to the front door. A hefty stone crown roof above, the building resembles a courthouse. Immediately inside, at a battered desk, sits a plump bespectacled crone. Behind her is a wide-open main room evidently given up to the needs of small children, cluttered with bright red and yellow plastic furniture; unkempt toys were strewn around.

Darting left I trotted up the circular staircase, reaching a turret-tower of a room topped by a splendid painted cupola. It might have been rather good looking some time long ago but now the windows are murky, the carpets shabby. The bookcases are ugly, free standing wood boxes dividing up the room like spokes of a bicycle wheel. I perused the shelves. Two girls, high school students I surmised, sat silently across from each other at a tattered table, notebooks splayed open, backpacks a-tumble on the floor, draining the sera of winter snowmelt.

I was halfheartedly dragging a gloved fingertip across grimy spines when suddenly I came across a trove of true crime books. Manna. My mind was made up, I had to enroll.

52

Giddy, I jogged downstairs to the frosty librarian, "How long does it take to become a member?" I asked, foisting electric bills in my name at her.

"Are you a homeowner, or are you renting?" she asked.

"Neither." I said, undaunted and shoved my bills across her desk. But she was not interested in my bills. She wanted to see a lease.

"It's policy."

Patiently, I explained that I have no lease. I am staying in the house of a friend. I have transferred the utility bills into my name because I am conscientious and decent and reliable, exhibiting exactly the type of appealing traits necessary to join her estimable institution. "I can't help you," she snipped. "Policy requires you show me a lease."

Turning her back to me she displayed a frosting of dandruff across her shoulders. I watched her for a while, waiting for her to swivel and yell, "April Fool's Day! Gotcha! Smile you're on Candid Camera." Instead, her cell phone burped and she picked it up and launched into a private conversation.

I was crushed by this rejection, and with no further options I slunk slowly homebound. Engrossed in private fulminations I concluded there must exist a connection twixt this absurd misadventure and America's abysmal literacy rate. Possibly, if I was a parent I would have felt duty-bound to dedicate myself to the rallying of reforms and the raising of public awareness. Instead I retreated to the comfort of my cozy rental.

Happy Ending

K-MART, IN ITS BRILLIANCE, offers a "Money Back Guaranteed Read." Certain volumes of the selection of fiction and non-fiction books have huge round egg-yolk yellow stickers with monster font advertising this deal of the century. "What is this all about? Do I get my money back if I don't like the ending?" I cozied up to a young female store clerk. "If I don't like the characters, or the plot? What is the refund based on?" No store employee knew anything about the details, nor was there any literature on the matter to shed light on exactly how this good time is guaranteed.

I ventured over to the Customer Service desk. A customer was already at the counter. She was hurling abuse at the calm employee behind the cash register;

Viviane, according to her nametag. Despite being on the slender side, the enraged customer had no trouble thrusting a dark green plastic sun chair at Viviane, no doubt to amplify her point. Loosely, her point was a threat that "they had just lost a really, really, really good customer." The customer cursed, she accused, she threatened. Her shrillness got to me and I soon found her rather annoying. With the sun chair held tightly against her flat chest, she made to swan off.

"See ya!" I barked, audibly.

Spinning around she focused all her attention on me. She squinted her eyes. "What did you say?" She asked, perhaps expecting me to combust from fear. She appeared to be in the habit of easily frightening others. Most likely she runs a school.

"I said, see ya!" And I flashed my most insincere smile. She stalked off.

After sharing the laugh of victorious warriors, Viviane told me not to worry about the Money Back Guarantee sticker on the book. "You don't need a reason. We take anything back."

Account Abuse

WHEN THE OFFICE-SOFT BANK MANAGER ASKED ME for my Social Security Number I fell into temptation and switched up a couple of the digits. I'll blame my childish behavior on healthy curiosity. I've been asked this number all my life, for one reason or another, and I've always told the truth. This was more social experiment than outright (potentially felonious) fib.

I was there to open an account. Mr. Peter, the bank manager, gathered my pertinent stats and tapped away at the keyboard of his computer. Directly after giving him the incorrect information there began a gnashing of teeth from behind Mr. Peter's desk. Sliding out from a fax machine came a page, like a tongue. Mr. Peter threw his left arm out and snatched the page without so much as turning in his chair. Must receive a lot of faxes, I figured. He grazed the page with a quick look, and then he froze. Mr. Peter was no longer typing. He was now very deliberately and carefully re-reading the piece of paper in his hand. A glistening of sweat spread over his face like morning dew.

Surreptitiously he tried to check me out. He cast furtive glances as I skittered nervously in my chair. My experiment was clearly going awry. His was not a look that screamed sexual harassment. Rather, it appeared as if he thought he might be in danger of physical harm. I started to sort out an alibi should my trick tumble any further south. Mr. Peter was now flashing crazy looks my way. "Anything wrong?" I asked while trying to sound mighty blasé, despite worries of life-long incarceration.

"Have you ever lived in Ohio?" Mr. Peter managed to stutter, turning pink, over-heating like a boiling lobster. Turns out the person to whom my switcheroo SSN belongs is wanted by the Feds. He is on record for Account Abuse. I don't know more as the perspiring Mr. Peter refused to up any extra details.

"Gosh!" I said, as, with grace, I extricated myself from any ties to this cheapening scene. I blamed the numbers error entirely on dyslexia. I would like to think I've learned a valuable lesson about the importance of telling the truth.

Sex for Free

THERE'S A RUMOR GOING AROUND that men are not getting enough sex. This is all being blamed on the cost of dating, of wining and dining. Getting a girl out of her pants the old fashioned way, by paying for it, one way or another. But with no cash, what's guy to do? Drama Boy, we'll call him, is a true Darwinian, and he has adapted. He's in his mid 30s, with sexy, lupine eyes, and an aura of melancholy. When he lost his flash job, so too went his portfolio of easy girlfriends. "So I got a little creative with my presentation. And—", he claims, "I can pull chicks like I used to."

Drama Boy developed a theory based entirely on exploiting the female predisposition for empathy. Sympathy sex.

He does in fact live in a brick-and-mortar house (rental), and has a job (retail): he reveals none of this. Instead, on any given Saturday night, he will stroll along Main Street, and hunt. Matter of time, and he'll spotlight a weak gazelle. The female is incapable of resisting sweet-talk. Using flattery you effectively sink a claw into her hind flank and grapple her to the ground. You run the show with the "where are you froms" and "what do you dos."

Once she is properly engaged, Drama Boy will let slip his recent tragic losses. Domicile, security, a future with the light on. Tears coil into her trusting eyes. He will tell her he hasn't eaten in days. Prey will feed him. Post repast, with Drama Boy in the passenger seat of Prey's luxury motor, she'll offer to take him home. Denouement.

"I have no home." Baleful expression expertly cast. "I've been living under the bridge. It's not as bad as you'd think." Drama Boy invites her to see his encampment. She is as repulsed as she is eager to earn her merit badge as a Samaritan. And there, under the stars, and the traffic noise on the bridge, Prey will put out like never before. She is all the more sensual for believing she is doing a good thing. Making someone's life a little better. The economy of seduction.

Melissa

IN THE MID-1970s my father rented a beach house in Southampton. I was seven years old at the time. The house was named, Barn Yesterday. Black letters painted on a white cross, planted in the crushed shell and pebble driveway where it met with the street.

My best friend was a girl named Melissa. She was my coloring, shape and size. We were bookends in our looks and even more so in our personalities. Her family was in a house nearby and every day we cavorted. We constructed cities from the sand, we made up languages, we hid in the Kelly green fronds of the dunes and stared, fascinated at the pages of my father's copies of Playboy.

We were a club of two and we vehemently denied membership to my siblings and hers.

At night, if the parents were gone to their cocktail parties, Melissa and I would throw ourselves into the swimming pool and practice staying under water as long as possible or lie around on the lawn and wait to see shooting stars. Or catch moon bugs in jars. Ordinary childhood pursuits.

Another pastime was to dress up in every piece of clothing we could find until we were bulky clowns. I had forgotten this game until I came across a Polaroid. In the picture we are festooned with mismatched layers and our underwear for hats. Our arms are slung across one another's shoulders, we are grinning.

Scholastic schedules being what they were, Melissa and I only had the summers to spend together. Three months of untrammeled fun, after which it was time to go back to school. I returned to England and Melissa to New York City. We hated the cruel separation.

"Wish we were sisters," we agreed.

On the last night of the holidays, when we were 9 years old, we wrote our wills. "In case something happens." This was Melissa's idea. It was a game to us. We were laughing from the moment we set pen to paper. Finally, we rolled the documents into tubes and secured them with black ribbon. We stashed them where we thought they would be safe.

One afternoon in October when I was home in London, my mother asked me to take a walk with her.

"Do you remember your friend Melissa?" My mother asked.

"Yes!" I said excitedly. I figured this meant Melissa was coming to visit.

"She died," my mother said. I yanked my hand from my mother's. My mother explained how an ember from the fireplace caught on the carpet and the house burned down. Melissa's mother and father escaped. But she and her little sister were stuck in their bedroom. Her mother went back inside and all three of them never made it out.

"Don't worry Darling, they didn't feel a thing," my mother said. I stared at the ground. "They died from the smoke."

Today I drove past Barn Yesterday and to my surprise it is torn down. All that remains is a shallow pit and a couple of contractors vans parked in the driveway. From the street I can see the dunes and the ocean beyond. The little name sign is gone.

I long ago lost my copy of the will I wrote with Melissa. The great sadness of her death morphed imperceptibly into a secret super-human strength for me. If I'm scared, I'll call out her name, and sure enough I instantly feel safe.

Who Goes to the Hamptons for the Winter?

WHO GOES TO THE HAMPTONS FOR THE WINTER? Me. I recently made

a deal with a charming devil and agreed to a house-sitting gig in the Hamptons.

To keep myself occupied and out of trouble I started poking on-line with regards

to possible employment. Most of the villages out here have shuttered Main

Streets, at least half the boutiques and fancy food shops are closed. The

Hamptons are a dismal place in the wintertime. Nevertheless, I thought I'd best

find myself some way to pay the gas company, et al.

Craigslist.com job possibilities for eastern Long Island suggested very

little of interest. I answered the first five listings regardless of type. I inquired

after the position of Tarot card reader to entertain at an upcoming charity fundraiser for autism on Staten Island. I asked about a job to play the victim in a TV re-enactment of a true crime murder filming in East Hampton at the end of January.

I heard back from the autism charity and Scott gave me a test and made me do a reading for him. This was all by email so I felt emboldened, at least up until Scott Facebooked me and asked me my age! I gave him some grief about the age question, but mostly because I needed to throw him off his game while I invented some hocus pocus for the card reading. I waited a few minutes and then I wrote him a paragraph on his relationship with his ex making sure to avail myself of all manner of clichés "trust your instincts," "follow your heart" and other beauties. I sent him my assessment of his romantic status and I never heard from him again.

Of course I got side-tracked and checked out the personals. I justified this time wasting/absorbing activity with the notion I needed acquaintances in this barren chilly land. For heteros there was only one single page. But there were copious ads for men looking for men—many attached with photographs of their manhood. Four listings for women looking for paid interaction. And Ben, a single dude who was howling at the virtual night sky, pining for his lost lady love. Ben wrote he'd forgo a million dollars just to have her in his arms again. My guess is no one has ever offered Ben a million dollars, else he'd know better.

Changing tack I looked at other people's job searches and offered employment to "famous guy needs work." I hankered to know how he was famous and why he was looking for work on Craigslist. But he turned out to be a fraud just like myself because after a couple of emails back and forth he admitted he was not famous and had been concerned no one would have responded to him if he wrote "total nobody needs job." I told him he was absolutely right and to high tail it out of my inbox.

Dan Aykroyd

FRIDAY EVENING AT A RESTAURANT IN EAST HAMPTON, I walked in on the improbable vision of Dan Aykroyd working behind the bar. He shook a silver shaker and passed out rounds of triangle-shaped goblets of fluid bliss to awestruck spectators. He was in town to promote his new line of brew, Crystal Head Vodka.

I went over to say hello and he introduced me as Foxenberg. Gotta love it! Dan emanates a humble, infectious contentedness and, along with his elixir, a merry time was had. And the martinis were delicious. Turns out Dan was in town for a variety of reasons, one being to ride the lead motorcycle and guide a parade for the Soldier Ride that honors America's wounded warriors. This is a huge local happening.

The parade of motorbikes, bicycles, strollers, walkers and the Head Mobile (the Crystal Head Vodka official motor coach) would slither from Amagansett to Sag Harbor and ultimately wind up in Montauk.

Before leaving the East Hampton restaurant that night Dan invited me to ride on the back of his Harley at the parade. I actually jumped in place at this invitation of the century. Dan said, "just be at the fire house in Amagansett, at 9:00 a.m. tomorrow."

What I did not say out loud was, "Hi, my name is Christina, & I'm an insomniac." Instantaneously, I activated panic mode at the thought of being anywhere at 9:00 a.m. I dashed home to a bottle of sleeping pills. The pills did nothing. Dread grew. I took more pills. Inevitably I did sleep, very deeply.

It was mid-afternoon when I awakened. I'd missed everything, and I felt a profound regret. What a friggin' loser was I? I tracked Dan down at a liquor store in Amagansett. I intended to apologize for my no-show. At the liquor store Dan sat behind a wood barrel and charmingly conversed with mesmerized vodka purchasing fans. The potato-juice is sold in bottles shaped like skulls, you'd think they would be macabre; but instead they are beautiful and witty.

Without compunction I lied and told Dan I didn't show up because I never in a million years thought he was serious. I didn't have the nerve to admit I over-dosed myself on sleeping pills. To my astonishment Dan told me my failure to appear was a good thing! He explained he had to steer the hog at parade speed and it would have been hard for him to manage with my additional weight. I ignored the implication of the mass of my ass.

In a flash I saw it. Bugles would have been bugling. Marines and veterans in attendance. I saw myself hopping onto the back of a shiny motorcycle bearing our visiting super-star Dan Aykroyd. And then I saw us tumbling to the tarmac, on account of my own self. I am in awe of our soldiers and would have had to kill myself if I had mangled their special day. Everything had worked out perfectly. I almost fainted with relief.

Dusk was nestling into shadows and it was time for Dan to go perform at the Wounded Warrior fund-raiser concert. Without hesitation he surged with notable fortitude into the motor coach Head Mobile. I asked him where he gets the energy to forge through such grueling days.

"I feel like I've been run over by a truck," he said. We rumbled off-road, down trails switching left and right through the gangly East End forest. We were in the backwoods of the Springs where it was moonless and shadow-filled and Steven King-creepy.

And then flood lights came looming out of the dark, and I could see the outlines of a tent, white peaks pulled tight, a flimsy roof hanging over a thick group of dazzling young faces. All of them solid-looking and intense. I noticed one handsome fellow walking with an almost imperceptible limp, my eyes gazed down to acknowledge an artificial lower leg. My heart exploded for him. I was paralyzed by the enormousness of what it all means and I could not look at him again.

The band Booga Sugar was on the stage, everyone in position, belting out something noisy. Dan stormed up, and the crowd boomed. Dan slammed right into a song, he is a big man and he can dance like you wouldn't believe. He went Cajun right before my eyes. Dan's magnificent perfectly rhythmic hips beat out the bass of the ditty.

I watched the faces of the soldiers. These young people looking at Dan, their eyes, bullets, fixed on him. I saw them, twenty, maybe thirty deep, at the front of the stage, comfortably pressing into an almost concrete throng. An entity of hopefulness, and scrubbed youth, and ravaged possibilities.

Dan delivered the goods as only he could have. Those beautiful boys and girls, men and women, were lifted from the heaviness if only for the length of time they watched wonderful Dan give them that diversion of joy. And he did. I saw the glow on the faces of those soldiers, sort of a reverie. It was magnificent.

Game Anyone?

OVERNIGHT THESE HAMPTONS, which I inhabit, have transformed into their familiar paradise. The landscape turned from taupes to a multiplicity of greens. Even the tree limbs are suddenly upholstered in soft fuzzy mosses. From my backyard I see fields of downy shrubs and tall golden ferns, which blur into a horizon of sunlight. Sights more ravishing than I can even remember. Breezes are playful and sensuous, and should it rain even the raindrops are juicy and soft and warm, they create a perfect percussion. It is sublime. People have popped out of nowhere; the empty houses have come back to life with lamplight blazing in the windows, smiling out on the end of a day, ready to reel in the dusk. Everywhere seems so inviting, welcoming.

Yet the beauty is no match to the inimitable perversities of my human nature, and I draw the shades. Ensnaring my laptop I retreat to bed; and then I give in—so sweet—to the quicksand-seduction of online gambling. In particular, backgammon. You don't even need a friend in the world and still you'll always get a game. The site kicks you off with 300 points. Highest stake is 200 points per game with a 40-point pot. There are many smaller pots to choose from. Here I am a shame-faced chicken and I always go for the smallest risks, even though it's not real money. Some competitors have scores in the tens of thousands. I'm no mathematician, but at approximately 15 minutes per game, that's a fairly macho quantity of, uh, "flight time."

The other evening, instead of accomplishing something productive, I started to play backgammon. I crashed from a high of just over two thousand points and tumbled almost without cessation to somewhere in the thirteen hundreds. Hours were chewed up by the half-dozen before I dragged my eyes from the laptop to take a quick read on whether it was day or night. Meanwhile nothing else got done. I'd not showered, nor left the house.

All of a sudden it was dawn and I was having trouble clearly seeing the computer screen. I could hardly even shove my now sticky stubborn mouse. Opponents wrote me glib jibes telling me I was an "idiot" for my molasses-slow moves. I knew I should stop, but I couldn't. It took falling asleep over the keyboard for me to quit the game.

Yesterday when I logged on I was stumped to find out I had won a lot of points during my previous coma-play. I was now back up to just under sixteen hundred points. The only thing I'd known for sure was that I could no longer see. Curiously this had no impact on my skill level. Whatever! I fell in lock-step with my addiction, and once again started to play, for hours. That is until I was interrupted by the familiar noise of those blasted morning birds. Dawn again! The sun was rising on another glorious day. I know I should go engage, I know I shouldn't give in so readily to my socio-agoraphobic inclinations. Except that I do. It is so easy to conjure vivid views of the highway and the back roads all clogged, bumper to bumper with the "summer people." I shudder and snuggle tighter with my laptop. It's back to the game for me.

A Final Fling

WE ALL KNOW WHAT MEN MEAN by a fun bachelor party, but women's freewheeling blowouts are still evolving. A decade or so ago the standard bachelorette party involved a club with a male revue, but—aside from stuffing bills into a dancer's G-string—the bride having physical contact with men other than the groom-to-be was rare. More recently these sendoff parties have become a booming business, with nightclubs and cruises that cater to both bachelors and bachelorettes popping up all over. And many women are jumping at the chance for a final fling. "I went to an overnight party on a small cruise ship," says one 25-year-old woman, "There were a few bachelorette groups and a couple of bachelor parties, and there were a lot of couples hooking up. I know one bride had sex with the best man from another party right on the deck."

Despite the growing popularity of specialty spots for such festivities, any public place is fair game for modern bachelorettes. Groups of women are turning up in trendy clubs, working-class restaurants, and bars in upper-class neighborhoods. "I was at a quiet lounge-style bar on the upper east side," says a young woman from New York City, "and there was a group of girls in their 20s celebrating at the next table. When I asked who the bride was, one of them pointed to a girl at a small table by the bar who was sitting with two guys. I did a double take and realized that both men had their pants open and she was giving one of them a hand job. After he came, she started on the other. By the time I left an hour later, she had jerked off about a dozen guys."

Of course, some girls just want to have fun. There are a number of websites that specialize in supplying treats for parties (including phallic food and ice-cube trays that make penis-shaped cubes), as well as an array of imaginative games. If you're lucky you'll go out one night and encounter a woman whose friends are making her play Buck a Suck, which requires the bride to wear a T-shirt with candy stuck all over it. The bachelorette will charge guys a dollar to suck a candy ($2 for strategically placed sweeties). Or the bride might be wearing a candy necklace as a low-riding belt; she has to invite men to eat the candy off. Another pastime involves handcuffing the bride to a naked male blow-up doll.

Her assignment is to beg items of clothing from strangers and try to get her "date" dressed by the end of the night. (Pin the Macho on the Man is best played in the comfort of someone's home. $10 buys a poster of a sexy stud and 15 cutout cocks.)

The classic entertainment at a house party will be a male dancer, but for him to strip down to a G-string isn't enough. Women are requesting dancers who do full nudity. Sean Casey, 28, who has worked for seven years as a stripper/wrestler in Cincinnati, says, "Women are getting crazier."

But according to Scott Layne, a former Chippendale's dancer who currently owns and runs Hollywood Men, Inc., a Los Angeles male revue, things haven't changed that much. He says, "When I was dancing in the 1970s women were crazy. As soon as they are away from men and in a safe environment, they cut loose. A man would be arrested for the things the ladies do. They tug on your G-string, grab and pull, flash their breasts."

The big difference is that now women are grabbing dancers in the relative privacy of a small party. So what's going on behind closed doors? Danny, the manager of Centerfold Strips in Mineola, Long Island, New York, encouraged me to talk to two of his popular guys, Dino and Russell.

Dino, 24, saw a movie when he was a teenager about a guy who became a dancer. He thought it looked cool, so he trimmed down and tried it out. "The first time I danced, my heart was in my throat," he tells me. "But I made $150 in

20 minutes. After that I was hooked. I've been dancing for 4 years. I intended for this to be my last year, but I still need the money. I'm in school studying pre-med. I make at least $400 to $500 a week." Dino, who lives with his parents, also does magic shows so his folks think that's how he makes his money. One evening I followed Dino on his rounds; he had 4 parties scheduled. (He says he puts 500 miles on his car every weekend.)

Bethpage, Long Island, 8:00 p.m.: Megan is throwing a bachelorette party for her good friend Caitlin. Dino is meant to be a surprise, so he meets Megan outside. Money changes hands up front, and Megan and I take Dino's boom box so she can cue his entrance. Inside, the dining table is laden with penis-shaped food. The party consists of ten pretty Irish girls in their early 20s, wearing leather and lots of black. They sip beer and chatter excitedly. The living-room furniture has been moved back against the walls, and Caitlin is seated on a chair in the center of the room. The first track is the theme song to the TV show Cops. "Bad boys, bad boys, watcha gonna do...?" Dino struts in dressed as a cop, and the women erupt with shrieks.

Dino takes Caitlin by the hand and throws her up against the wall to be frisked. The girls scream, Caitlin giggles. Dino puts Caitlin back in her chair, then unzips her knee-length black boots and throws them to the floor (Caitlin is embarrassed by her thick white socks). Dino thrusts his crotch in her face and wiggles fast; more screams, Caitlin laughs. Dino bops away and removes his shirt. The girls shriek.

The next song is Joe Cocker's "You Can Leave Your Hat On." Dino bends over with his buttocks directed at his audience, then pulls his pants off. He is now naked except for boxer shorts, boots, and his hat. He dances with Caitlin, tugs her close, grabs her by the waist and propels her into the air. She is no longer nervous. She is having a great time.

Then Dino goes around to all the guests, pulling them up to dance with him. One girl is too shy to get up, so he grabs her beer bottle, holds it as if it's his penis, and encourages her to drink. He bumps and grinds in their faces, drapes his shirt over their heads and simulates getting felatio. Dino finally removes his boxers, revealing a tiny red G-string on his shaved, tanned, and toned butt, and the women scream again. Half of them are up dancing and rubbing against him, folding dollar bills into his G-string.

The next stop is a house on a leafy residential street in Queens. It is 9:30. Dino collects his fee, then hands over the boom box so he can make his big entrance, but no one seems to know where to plug it in. Dino comes in, struts around the living room; the women scream madly as he leans over the back of the sofa in search of an outlet. Before his show has even begun, the audience is hysterical. Except for grandma, who is sucking on her teeth in an unpleased way.

"Bad Boys" comes on and Dino starts his show. He pats down Karen, the bride-to-be. With his crotch in her face, he slides a wooden baton between his legs and again simulates getting felatio. Karen is laughing, with her hands in front of her face. A raunchy aunt gets in on things, aggressively leading Dino by the hand. But he is skillful, moving from one girl to another and always returning to Karen. One girl gets caught up in a bawdy dance. She ends up with her pants down around her ankles and her white-thonged booty twitching in frenzy. Grandma leaves the party, shaking her head with dismay.

Dino is lost in the mob of screaming girls, although they sit back down when he turns away. He is clearly enjoying himself, 'til a small child wanders in. Dino cringes until the child is removed. Lou Bega's "Mambo No. 5" plays several times while Dino dances with the girls, giving his phone number to the most outgoing.

We arrive at the next house, also in Queens, at 11. A swarm of young and middle-age Latinas await our star. The place is decorated with giant penis-shaped piñatas, a table is spread with phallic cakes and cookies, the drinks have penis shaped straws. "Bad Boys" starts and Dino does his thing. Everything is great until I kick the extension cord and unplug the boom box. Dino, mid-thrust, is forced to stop and plug it back in. The music starts again, but Dino has lost his flow. When he approaches one woman she just stares at him, unsmiling and a tad hostile. Dino moves on to another woman. He says, "You look like an orange. Can I peel you?" She is not amused.

Finally Dino takes one of the penis piñatas and dances around with it, holding it like it's a giant erection. There are a few randy girls but not enough for Dino; he wraps up more quickly than usual, happy to get out of there.

At midnight we are in the Fordham University section of the Bronx, and a wild party is in progress. Men and women hang out on the stairs, on the porch, in the street. The apartment has very little furniture and nothing on the walls, mattresses on the floor, balloons hanging from the ceiling. This is a combination bachelorette and birthday party. Many young children are rushing around, and women are screaming at the kids, herding them out of the living room. As soon as Dino parks his car, the party is abuzz that "El Muchacho" has arrived.

Dino goes into a back bedroom while 35 or so women gather in the front room. "Bad Boys" starts and the crowd roars with appreciation. Dino makes his entrance. He begins with the bride-to-be, but is instantly surrounded by the women. The few men who stayed to watch now leave, and the ladies go mad. They are all up and dancing around Dino, pulling at his thong and stuffing in dollar bills. Eventually they go too far and he has to call a time-out.

The wildest girl, young with a good figure, is barefoot and wearing a tight skirt and a halter top. She stops Dino, then does a handstand in front of him, lining up her crotch with his, and puts her ankles in his hands. Her hips start vibrating like a power tool. Dino continues to dance, and she gyrates with him, her eyes glowing. When Dino finally lets go and sits on a chair, the girl pulls her skirt off and jumps into his lap. She pulls her lacy white thong to one side and grinds her butt into him. 15 other girls are swarming him, all wanting a turn on his lap. The white thong girl spins away, misty-eyed, and dances around by herself in her tiny underwear. A friend motions to her that she is crazy, she laughs and smacks her own backside.

Outside later, Dino says that was one of the wildest gatherings he's ever seen. "Those girls wanted cock," he says. "They were aching for it, and I got in the mood too. The heat of the moment is hard to resist if you're a normal guy. This is a great way to make money, but it's a strange altered reality."

And then I met Russell. To hear him tell it, plenty is happening, sometimes even enough to warrant calling off the wedding. "Depending on the type of girl, it can get raunchy," he says. "At one bachelorette party, this girl I met said, "I'm never going to see you again. You're probably attracted to me, I'm attracted to you, so let's just do it.' I said, 'Do you have a condom?''

Russell agrees to talk with me, but only if I meet him in person. He lives in the house he grew up in, a roomy home on a pretty street with trees and tidy lawns. He is tall and hunky with a young-looking face, dark hair, and pouty lips. I follow him upstairs and see that his jeans are tight on his firm legs, his ass solid. A landing leads to his bedroom, with plain walls and a twin bed in one corner, a computer and entertainment equipment, a closet full of Gap-simple clothes, tags still on. A spent condom and a pile of clothes sleep on the floor.

"Recently I went to a club upstate," he begins. "A crappy little place, with three old guys sitting at the bar. One guy says, 'have a good time,' and points to another room. I poked my head in, and 350 girls started screaming. As soon as I started my act these girls were tearing off my clothes, pouring whipped cream on me, trying to go down on me. Everyone was touching me. It was like a rape scene. I was underneath them. There were hands everywhere, a tongue down my throat, someone stuck a finger in my ass. I could not get up. I didn't want to hurt them by throwing them off, but it was overwhelming. Finally one of them said, 'Let him get up.'

"After the show, groups of girls were fighting over who I was going home with. I left with 16 of them. I put on a condom, and I had a great time. It was a huge orgy. I would finger the girls first to get them wet, then I had sex with one girl, pulled out, put it in another girl. I had sex with 16 different girls. Some girls were half-dressed, some were naked, and some were fingering themselves. One girl was so hot, blonde and tanned, and I had anal sex with her. I don't usually do that with someone I don't know well. She loved it."

The clothes on the floor turn out to be Russell's costumes. "When I come into a party I wear a suit. I want to come in like somebody's husband, like wouldn't it be nice if just once your husband came in looking like me." He pulls out a pair of black pants and shows me the Velcro that permits him to rip them off at the right moment. He says, "I have found everything in my G-string from a $100 bill to a K-Mart coupon."

He pops a video into the VCR, and I see shaky shots of him and two other male strippers entertaining a roomful of women in a hotel convention room in Manhattan. The men shimmy down to their skivvies and move in close to the shrieking ladies. Russell swivels his crotch inches from one women's face, then hops onto a table to better gyrate at eye level. He informs me, "It's a big no-no to spill anyone's drink."

There are plenty of rules by which a dancer must abide. Diets are strict and managers merciless. The body needs to be perfectly toned, muscles ripped and cut, body hair shaved, tan bled in. Pulling at a millimeter of excess flesh at his midriff, Russell says, "My manager won't let me dance looking like this."

But there are plenty of incentives to maintain that perfect exterior. "4 girls will give me a blowjob at the same time," Russell tells me. "My guy friends tell me I'm lucky, but I say, fuck you. You go to the gym every day.'

"When I first come out, a lot of the women yell. Once I'm in my G-string and they know they're going to get a chance to touch me, they get quiet. They stare. Some try sticking their hands under my G-string. The really horny ones will try to stick their face in my crotch. It's $275 for 20 minutes of dancing, but I don't charge more even if I stay longer.

"I charged a girl $400 for sex once," Russell continues. "I was finished dancing at a club and this girl was following me around the whole night. I wasn't into her, so I tried to blow her off, but she wouldn't go. At the end of the night she said, 'why don't you come home with me?' I said, 'Well, it's not going to be free.' She said, 'I'll give you anything you want, and I'll give you a blowjob if you want that.' So I threw out an outrageous figure because I didn't think she'd go for it. I said, 'Four hundred dollars for a blowjob, and then I have to go. I'm running late.' She took me home."

But it's not all fun and games for Russell: "One time I went home with a pig. It was the end of a gig and there was one gross fat chick hanging around. She said, 'You can come to my house, I live a block away.' I was so tired, I went. I sat on her bed, then she undressed me the way a mom would. I was practically sleeping, and she was going down on me. I could barely keep it up. Then I saw her trying to straddle me, so I said, 'Aren't you forgetting something?' And she took about an hour trying to get the condom on because I couldn't keep it up. I said, 'It's not you; I'm just exhausted.' She gave me a blowjob, but I couldn't come. I stopped her, but her head stayed down there, so I masturbated while she watched and I kind of got it on her.

"Right at that second, reality hit," Russell continues. "I was really tired, it was five in the morning, this girl was really gross, and this house was totally falling down. So I got up and said, 'I've got to go,' just like a girl. I left in my G-string and my boots, pulling my clothes on. She said, 'Don't you want my number?' I said, 'Oh shit, of course, I should have asked.' I'm not out to hurt anybody."

When I ask Russell if I can accompany him on his round of bachelorette parties and see his act for myself, he says I can come if I agree to go home with him at the end of the night. "You mean I have to have sex with you?" I ask, flattered. "Yes," he says. "It's going to get really hot and intimate, and I can't have you watching without getting involved. It's not fair to anyone. Especially your boyfriend."

Oh yeah, him. I decline the offer. And if I do get married, there'll be no wild partying for me.

Oh Shit

HAVE YOU HEARD THE STORY of the tuna and the shark? There was a large, very old tuna that lived in the deep sea, somewhere mid-ocean. He had lived there all his life. Along came a shark, sly and slippery and dark. With great speed, the shark lunged at the venerable tuna and ripped free a mouthful. The shark motored on, his slim mouth full of fish flank. The tuna was stunned. He could see the gaping hole left in his side. He was too shocked to feel the pain, yet.

The tuna floundered. He was faced with the sight of his own mortality. For all his wisdom, and for all his years, he had never expected to go out in such a drab, commonplace way.

The shark moved with tremendous power and he was soon almost indiscernible. Only the flicker of his tail was visible, propelling him forward on his journey.

The tuna was left alone. His side hurt like a mother. Threads of bloodied filaments followed his every move like the tendrils of a man-o-war. He remembered stories he'd heard of other tunas that'd been attacked by predators. He knew of several who had survived such calamities. He consoled himself with fabled tales of wounded fish, veterans of the water-wars.

He looked about for the shark, and only barely was able to make out a flash of the shark's rudder of a tail. It was vanishing into the distance.

He sighed, carefully, and marshaled his confidence. Apparently this particular tuna had always been an optimist and he decided he was going to survive. He was going to lick his wounds and get on with living. But then something caught his attention. A movement, a glint in the inky waters. Something far away was astir. The tuna strained to see what it was. It was the shark. Slowly, but surely, he was turning around. The shark was coming back...

As the Montauk fishermen told me, this is what they call an "oh shit" story.

Some Fish

YESTERDAY, LATE IN THE AFTERNOON, I was walking along the shore of a bay. A movement out on the water caught my attention. I couldn't make it out as the sun was directly behind it. Whatever it was, it was shuddering noisily with speed. Clattering and zooming into view it turned out to be a Sunfish sailboat.

In an instant the vessel was vertical and the dude aboard was standing up with the little boat traveling behind him, like a wall. The mariner was grappling with the ropes and a crazily flapping sail. Full speed, sliding over the water, he was headed for land and, slowly I noticed, I was directly in the way.

Panic.

Heart racing, I clumsily attempted to scarper in the direction of the dunes. But the Sunfish was too quick and it struck the beach, right at my toes. I held my breath, but just as suddenly, the boat was all innocence. Not so much as a whisper from the sails. The monstrous danger evaporated into the original perfect sunshiny afternoon.

Up close I could see the young man in charge was no more than a boy, maybe 14 years old. He hadn't seemed to notice me at all. Our parallel realities related only in their intensities. He stayed sitting on the now tranquil tub, ran a hand through tangled hair.

Then he started yelling: "I was pissing in my pants in the whole time! I've never been more frightened in my whole life! That was great!"

Stars and Bars

LOS ANGELES IS THE SISTER CITY to Shangri-la, and its citizens would melt or evaporate if they left the safe confines and immediate swank environs of Beverly Hills. In 1996, what I saw of life in Los Angeles was like living out an episode of Melrose Place. Everywhere there was a steady stream of celebrity guest-appearances. Drai's, the hot restaurant of the month, was considered a morgue if Clint or Sylvester were not at least two plastic-surgeoned bodies away.

Parties are pockmarked with movie stars in such generous quantities it feels like a jaunt down an aisle at Blockbuster Video. When brawls break out, the participants could be Rod Stewart's then 13-year-old daughter Kimberly versus

Bijou Philips, offspring of one of the Mamas and Papas. And attempting to pry them apart might be junior stars like Leonardo Di Caprio and Ashley Hamilton, son of George.

A drive down Sunset Boulevard was likely to provide a titillating glimpse of Tommy Lee and his larger-than-life wife, Pamela Anderson, strolling along. Pamela, a shy filly, walks with her head down and her eyes up, a sly, seductive smile fleshing out her curvy lips, catching greedy looks.

Matt Le Blanc, the spike-haired pretty boy of *Friends*, buys his morning coffee at one of the several million Starbucks, the coffee-house chain that had just begun its viral spread. He does not shy from the whisperings and finger-pointing all around him. He sucks up the rewards of fame, somehow slowing down the hands of time, to better savor the 15 minutes.

The car of choice those days in Los Angeles was the Hummer, a "tank" almost twice as wide as a regular vehicle, with room for one passenger beside the driver, musical amplification that could compete with concerts at Wembley, and the all-important anti-aircraft rocket-launchers made popular by the scourge of drive-by shootings. Outside fashionable boutiques where appointments were required, parking signs read: "Hummer, BMW, Mercedes, Jaguar and Rolls-Royce only. All other cars will automatically explode."

I moved to Los Angeles in pursuit of that year's boyfriend, who, for the sake of the story, I will call Bud Weiser. I met Bud one winter when I was holed up in an attic in Sag Harbor, a deafeningly quiet former whaling village near the end of Long Island. During the summer months, Sag Harbor is abuzz with beach trippers, but the winter, which lasts an anti-seasonal nine months, is returned to the locals and their small-town peculiarities already deftly portrayed by the likes of Steven King.

Toiling at the computer, attempting to tap out the 400th draft of a manuscript almost lifeless from multiple wounds inflicted upon each and every sentence, frustration and near-total stasis was achieved. Thus Bud's uncanny appeal. When he threatened to drive away into the sunset, or rather directly to Sunset Boulevard, Los Angeles, I forgot about my commitments to my patient editor, reformatted my former loathing for all things Californian, and packed. I followed Bud's highly polished truck, equipped with a cooler and a thousand cans of beer. I floored my rattletrap Chrysler station-wagon trying to keep up, unmindful of the gross faux pas of inflicting such an un-chic machine on LA.

Lady Luck cast a casual eye in the direction of Bud and myself, and we met Red. Red is the wife of a member of a rock band—the bass player to be precise—and she lives in indolent splendor in a three-bedroom house slightly outside the walls of Bel Air. After just one meeting, Red invited us to move in, and so began the true Los Angeles experience.

Red lives with three dogs and a monstrously loud stereo system forever tuned into a German-Hip Hop station. A bizarre collection of 16-year-old girls—

children of the famous—wandered in and out, camped on the sofa or in the guest room for weeks at a time. I realized too late that writing was now permanently impossible. Round one to Bud.

Bass Man, Red's charming husband who paid the bills, would make an appearance thrice weekly after AA meetings and escort Red to the movies, fulfilling her meager obligations to insure the flow of cash. Bass Man makes few demands, but one "unnegotiable" was sobriety, this cramped Bud's style tremendously. Round two to me.

Red is an actress, though she neither acts nor attends auditions. She doesn't even have an agent. Illusion is the name of the game: lush gardens in the desert; mock-17th-century chateaux alongside mock-Palladian villas filled with exercise equipment and refrigerators with automatic calorie-counting sensors. The pose supersedes the action in Los Angeles, and he with the best pose wins.

Red was obsessed with a dark and beautiful basketball player, the star rebounder on the worst team in the NBA, who had just received $35 million and a contract. Bass Man joked that he believed his wife was converting, to become a negro. He'd say, "if Michael Jackson can become white, then why not?"

Bass Man was quite content to pay for obscenely expensive courtside tickets; however he was never invited to attend. Red's fixation led her, me and Bud to the Downtown Sports Arena for a number of games, where Red would cheer manically after asking, "Who made that point?" and "Should I clap?"

On the day of a game Red would drag herself out of bed sometime after three in the afternoon—early for her—and drive to Umberto's *the* salon at the epicenter of Beverly Hills. Here, her naturally curly and originally brown hair was painted the color of fire and stretched straight, molded into movie-star shape. Her make-up was applied, eyelashes were glued on, extra-long plum-colored nails affixed and after donning yet another brand-new Prada outfit, with shoes and handbag to match, she was ready to attend the ball game.

I was brought along in the role of beard, side-kick, companion, and make-up monitor, instructed to alert her the moment a shine broke through the heavy powder on her not-quite-perfect nose. That she has not altered her nose is a sign of supreme self-confidence, since there are no noses in Los Angeles. In fact, if you check the profiles at any given soiree, there will be no unsightly bumps in view. The only permissible protrusions are lower down, in silicone, and in pairs.

Despite these fabulous distractions and in the interest of meeting my contractual obligations regarding the book, I rented a home away from home where I installed my computer and my editor's notes and, daily, I further tortured the paragraphs of my manuscript. Meanwhile, Bud took a job as a bartender and started living on a similarly nocturnal schedule as Red, arising late in the afternoon: breakfasting as I (head throbbing and spent) returned from the writing hovel and tossed myself into bed.

Eventually, when my book was finished, I packed and padded out while the others slept and returned to the East Coast by air, leaving my highly embarrassing Chrysler station-wagon in the hands of a helpful Iowan prairie boy who, I hoped, would drive it to the shipper's. I doubted my room-mates would notice my departure until the rent came due.

Purple Bear

I WAS ON TIME, for once in my life, for dinner at the house of a new friend. I parked my car and without bothering to ring the doorbell, I barged in. A sullen quiet filled the foyer. The air smelled undisturbed, stale. The lights were off. There appeared to be no one home.

"Hello?" I called out. It has happened that I've messed up dates in the past, or gone to the wrong house entirely. There was no denying it, things weren't looking good. A door slammed, snapping my attention to the top of a flight of stairs. A man in a terry robe. Erik. My host.

"We said 7! It's only 6!" He cawed. "I still need to take a shower!" Inexplicably, he was clutching a purple teddy bear.

"No worries!" I lied quickly. "I've a got a quick errand that needs doing." To fill the hour I sat myself in a diner. The smells of cooking stirred my appetite and soon I buckled and ordered a cheese omelet. Time passed and I returned to my host's home to find the lights on, soothing music playing, and Erik ably manning pans in the kitchen. All was well. Except all was not well. Where was everyone else?

"I may have been early, but where are the others!" I asked.

"It's just us," said Erik. "My girlfriend is out of town."

"Brilliant." I said, thrown off completely. But, I rationalized, I'm a big girl, I have nothing to fear, I can handle this. The meal was consumed, compliments to the chef and all that. After dinner he invited me to join him on the sofa. Trying to act cool, I sat at the opposite end of the sofa, facing him. I was tucked as far back as I could get. But then he swiveled his body and suddenly he had his legs stretched out, covering most of the space between us. He started to thrum his be-socked feet against my thigh. I pretended this was not happening. His toes wiggled in some dingy mustard-colored socks. I pressed myself back against the armrest hoping to snatch an inch of space.

Erik excitedly jabbered on about some recent good fortune come his way, but I found myself distracted by these little bunny ears twitching beside me. Ratcheting up the affront, Erik suddenly grabbed my ankles and attempted to haul them into his lap.

"No!" I said, as I yanked myself from his grasp.

"I want to give you a foot rub!" Erik said, blushing. "And I want you to give me a foot rub. I love them!" He said, and pressed the awful socks against my thigh. I sprung to my feet. With giggles to help diffuse the awkwardness I excused myself. I was in my coat and out the door in the snap of a finger. It wasn't until the drive home I remembered the purple teddy-bear. I should have known right then. I should have known better than to return.

Blown Away

I MET A FRENCHMAN, named Norbert. We exchanged numbers and made a date for a drink at a bar in lower Manhattan. Half way through his glass of red wine, Norbert excused himself to go to the men's room.

On paper he wasn't atrocious. At least he hadn't asked to borrow money, yet. He claimed a craving to be a writer and was in our fair hamlet of New York City, far from his Parisian garret, to secure himself a publisher. Idling at the table for two, slurping from a Heineken, I pictured a life with Norbert. I could see us lounging on a lawn, a couple offspring chasing butterflies.

Norbert was gone a long time. I wondered if he had bladder issues. Could I cope with looking after him if his body caved to bad health? Norbert returned and flopped into the stained, crushed red velvet-backed chair. He was beaming.

"I ran into ze publisher cheek! Ze one ooo never returned my phone calls!"

"She must have liked you. You were gone for ages. Did you schedule a meeting?" I was pleased for him.

"She came wiz me to ze toilette," Norbert's voice was rising, a little shrieky. "She did me a blow job!"

I was even more pleased when I heard she never did publish his book.

Disco Discount

HAVE YOU EVER WONDERED where the 80s party people are? Probably you haven't given it a whole lot of thought. But consider the cultural impact as they seep out into the hinterlands, taking with them keepsakes of good times past.

For example, my friend Nalim, a glamour-God, who glammed it up from coast to coast on every continent, until one day when he felt decidedly burnt out. He relocated somewhere upstate New York. Far enough away to restore his health, while close enough to return to the trough of vice, should need be. When Nalim first arrived in his new hometown, and took his clothes to the dry cleaners, he was offered a 10% discount, a local tradition tendered to visiting entertainers, "they thought I was with the circus."

On Needs

I DON'T KNOW ABOUT YOU, but I need a cup of coffee first thing in the morning. When I awoke with fuzzy morning-eyes I scanned the room and got nothing I was in an unfamiliar bedroom, not for the first time I might add, but that would be another story. And not that I'm complaining, in this particular instance the bedroom I'm in is comfortable as a cloud.

I have no idea where I am. But I know that I need a cup of coffee so I best get on with figuring out my Global Position. No sound disturbed me, yet I awoke. It was all amorphous, woke up for the sake of needing no more sleep, thank you very much. A window was wide open, and all I could see was that it was dark outside. Warm and lovely inside. Even if I still had no idea where I was.

The red lights of an electric clock read "6:04." 6:04 what, though? I thought. Could as easily be dusk as dawn. No discernible clues to work with. I lay still. If it turned out to be early evening I'd make a mission of making a big night out of it. As a way to wisely use this seemingly extra-found time. If it was morning, which would mean I had been a-slumbering twelve hours straight, then I had probably best get my ass out of bed and fix on getting something productive done. Either way, by the looks of things, I would be getting out of these lover's arms of a tender bed. But what to do about the needed coffee? How do I get me some? When I still don't know where I am.

I lie unmoving in the snug bed, my eyes are closed. Letting the magic happen. And then I hear the sounds of a New York City garbage truck. The hydraulics, the dragon snort of exhaust, the men barking and slapping the side of the rig. Oddly sexy, those garbage collectors, but, as I'm known to say, that would be another story.

I open my eyes, I see daylight glowing its first shiny swipe, and indisputably it is day. I've had the almighty mother of naps and yes, I do feel a million bucks for it. More important, I know where I am. I am in NYC. And coffee will be a short walk away. I bound.

I'm out the front door and daylight has shot up another shade, to a milky grey with overtones so awesome they could only be captured by the brilliant Brit painter (whose name eludes me—lots of initials?). Never mind, his name is not important, only his oeuvre is important. Yet still his talent doesn't begin to compete with that of Mother Nature. In the warming glow of a glorious day I have walked to the corner where the street meets the avenue. No cars interrupt the rain-wet streets. I start to cross and watch a man, young, cherubic, somehow his aura reads "determined," and he has just finished running up the metal garage door front on the west side of his establishment. He is now charging around the corner to the adjoining south wall where he releases the metal door and runs it noisily upward, crashing it to its moorings. And I've only just arrived at the other side, stepped up onto the curb. The establishment is a coffee shop.

"Are you open?"

"Right this second," he says.

God I love New York.

Bio Haz

WHAT DO YOU THINK makes the perfect gift for Father's Day? How about DNA results? My own father, he who was married to my mother while I was conceived, likes to suggest that we are not related, his pet name for me is "the little bastard." Whether or not he is also implying that my mom is a ho, is another story.

In times of stress, for example, when I would ask my dad to bail me out of my gambling debts, he'd say, "Why should I support you? You don't look anything like me!" Before the advances in understanding of DNA the issue of illegitimacy was a deep sea to swim in. Most of the time my father and I got along just fine, and then it was a delight to believe I was genetically affiliated.

Conversely, when we squabbled and I could only see him as King Crab, I relished the alternatives.

There were times when he would call me "the little bastard," and I would pray to God that I was. Still, I always knew one day I would need to know for certain, whatever the results. Brave new modern age we live in, all things have become possible. And, lo, in Salt Lake City there is a lab that, for a measly $500, will untangle your double helix and provide definitive proof of who is, and who is not, your daddy.

I ordered a gift certificate from the lab, to pay for one paternity test. A buddy noted, "$500 for the DNA test. $50 for FedEx. Finding out you're not an Oxenberg—priceless." Ha ha ha. Well, better not repeat that to dad.

Today I phoned Daddy-O to tell him to expect a gift certificate in the mail. And, to wish him a "Happy Father's Day!"

As Seen on TV

A COURTROOM—Manhattan. March 2010.

The Judge: "Were you growing marijuana in your closet?"

The Defendant: "No Ma'am."

The Plaintiff: "He's lying! I have witnesses."

The Judge: "I'm gonna ask you again, were you growing marijuana in your closet?"

The Defendant: "No Ma'am. It was in the kitchen."

Curb Alert

SOME PEOPLE BELIEVE "you get what you pay for." Others say, "the best things in life are free." But what if you've recently lost your high-income job? What if your furniture was repo'ed by the rental company and you can't afford to replace it? Maybe your fiancé is threatening to seek love elsewhere now that you can't spring for the wedding of her dreams? Perhaps your so-called friends are no longer returning phone calls just as your financial wellbeing has started to come undone? Should you kill yourself?

Absolutely not. At least not account of insolvency. There are spoils a-plenty to be had on Craigslist for absolutely diddly-squat. Here are a few recent posts:

Need furniture?

…I think this couch may be the ugliest piece of furniture that has ever been created, from the fabric that screams... well, it just screams… to the fine sheet metal paneling on the front. I can't believe that someone actually built this thing. I live in a 4th floor walk-up & I'll happily help you move it.

Getting married?

…wedding gown, for a full figure gal, 5'5", 225lbs. Giving it away because I can't seem to sell it, even when I made it as low as 10 dollars. I am remarried now and, well, new hubby, new dress. It is in good condition. Maybe it needs a dry cleaning. Please be a female.

Want a friend?

…I have a turtle. I've had him forever. To mix up his diet I feed him live fish. It's recommended. But this one fish has managed to make friends with my turtle. Come to find out turtle bacteria and goldfish poop attract flies, so I've separated them. I'd hate to see him meet his fate with the toilet bowl. It would be awesome if someone would take Lucky, the goldfish, and give him a good home.

Want to get rid of that new friend?

..I found a small fish tank with a large crack in it.

And reminding one to stay alert on the virtual curb are creepy posts. like:
.. ladies. any of you want a sterling silver necklace? Free...

Creepy because legend has it if you want to catch a fish or a female shake something shiny.

Oh No He Didn't!

NO ONE LIKES a "smarty-pants," but sadly, someone has to don the duds. I have selflessly elected to sacrifice for the cause.

The other day, on TV, I was listening to a college professor (read: someone who SHOULD know better) discuss his thoughts on offshore banking and its potential illegalities. In his list of popular environs to stash cash out of the taxman's grasp, he included the Isle of Guernsey, which he pronounced "GW-ARN-SEY." It ought to be illegal to enrich someone so ill-equipped to educate.

No wonder Europeans (read: those who DO know better) condemn us Yanks to the Hall of Shame. I swiftly Googled the Prof, located an email address c o the college where he is heedlessly employed to steer the next generation into the abyss of assholery.

Driven purely by a desire to protect our great nation from further embarrassment, I explained how to pronounce the fiscally friendly little islets' name. "Like the cow." Oddly, I have not received the cloyingly grateful reply I anticipated—yet. Must be coming soon. I can't believe the Prof is both ignorant AND ill-mannered.

No doubt he will soon be asking for my help with Jethou, Brecqhou, Burhou, and Lihou prior to his next public foray.

New Jersey is Pro-Bush

LAST FRIDAY NEW JERSEY LAWMAKERS almost took an official vote to ban the Brazilian bikini wax. For clueless hirsute readers, the Brazilian wax job means not a hair is left in place. The ban was being considered by the state's Board of Cosmetology and Hairstyling because two women had been hospitalized last year after developing infections.

At the last minute New Jersey Consumer Affairs Director David Szuchman wrote: "I cannot agree to the complete prohibition...banning removal of hair in the genital area." So I guess now we know what he likes.

Not Catherine

THE MORE ELDERLY READERS AMONGST YOU may remember the 1980s and a TV confectionary treat of a show, a soap-opera of bubble bath proportions, "Dynasty." My older sister, Catherine Oxenberg, played a role. She absorbed all sorts of public adulation, and ever since then I've juggled the impact.

At the time, I was publishing my first book, *TAXI*, and I went straight to work folding Catherine's high profile into the machinations of my marketing schemes. My book was a collection of anecdotes of funny things that happen to people in taxicabs in New York City. I needed a contribution from my sister, obviously. For whatever reason she never could supply one. Now that I think about it, I should have expanded my search to include limousine misadventures. Anyway, since sister-Catherine did not supply I went boldly forth and invented a story for her. I'm pretty sure she didn't mind. And no one else would ever know. No harm done.

Catherine and I are very close in age. In every other aspect we are diametric contrasts. We always were this way. Pre-pubescent she cried in the rain, I jumped in puddles. She hoarded money, I tossed all my stuffed toys out the window of our home. Catherine wore French underwear from Harrods, it was a lucky day if my socks matched. We are still this way.

There are benefits to my one degree of separation to TV-stardom. I will confess that when it suited my purposes, I have gone so far as to say that I am Catherine. Like the time I booked a table at a fancy Los Angeles restaurant. I made a reservation for lunch for two, under my sister's name. I arrived first and was seated at a prominent booth, one of the "good" tables. A few minutes behind me was my lunch companion, Jasper, a very tall, very handsome African American gentleman. The maitre d'hôtel dawdled by and looked askance at us but managed to hold back from commenting. I pondered the legal ramifications on impersonating a celebrity.

Waiters cruised by darting disbelieving glances. I noticed them whispering to each other. I hoped Catherine didn't try to book a table here anytime soon. I felt a bit guilty. But only a bit.

Years back I was having a bad time of things. I had a job as researcher for a writer of non-fiction. My responsibilities included making cold calls to the sought-after well-to-do crowd. I left polite soft-voiced messages but no one called me back. So I got crafty and said the message was from Catherine. All my calls were immediately returned. One man went so far as to invite me to dinner which was a tricky unplanned-for challenge. Flummoxed, I was forced to confess I was a big fat liar and I was in fact Catherine's younger sister. Un-amused, the man un-invited me. Embarrassing, let me tell you.

Sometimes I find the mix-up amusing, like Steve-O who I've known going on 2 years and he still calls me "Cat-Reen," his version of the pronunciation. Other times it gets on my tits. For example, today I received a bill from the plumber and the invoice is made out to Catherine Oxenberg. I contemplated not paying the bill since it is not addressed to me. I fantasized marking the envelope "addressee not known at this residence."

To this day strangers pester me after her wellbeing, her whereabouts, and most specifically, "Is she still acting?" Usually these people have never met her. Gentlemen admit, "Don't hold it against me, but when I was in college I had a poster of your sister on my wall." Women are more aggressively inquisitive and drop three sometimes four questions on me all at once. Depending on the whim of the moment, so shapes my response. Occasionally I'll produce an honest reply.

But when I'm faced with a hard-ass busy-body nosy-parker, I have been known to say, "I don't know Catherine Oxenberg. Different family."

Do These Gloves Make My Ass Look Fat?

—How I got out of the wool business alive…

I COULD NEVER HAVE FORESEEN SUCH AN OUTCOME, but after 8 years selling clothing to women I felt sorry for men. The insecurities of women are staggering and ultimately embarrassing. I spent countless hours listening to females ranting plaintively about their body parts. It was the cost of doing business, I understood that, but increasingly it made me entertain tantalizing thoughts of suicide. They flapped at the injustice of fat thighs, limp skin or saggy butts as if they had no control over themselves. If I offered a sleeveless tank the answer was, "I never show my arms, I don't like them," or if I proffered a short skirt they'd say, "I have bad legs." All of them: fat, thin, toned or not, complained rigorously about the size of their ass.

Frequently they'd go so far as to grab what excess they could as if it were evidence in a trial. Excuses for imperfection were chucked about, everything from childbearing to boredom. Every single one of them was unhappy with the contour of their corps and I was forced to feign interest. For the sake of a sale I cooed compliments and reassurances. And finally I had to agree with men that all women are crazy when it comes to their personal body image.

Many years ago I wanted to be a writer. By some great good luck I met with a publisher who thought the same. After 2 books and still no income I had to cast about for other forms of employment.

In 2002 I had the dubious good fortune to meet with a fiber far softer than cashmere. The inner down of the Arctic musk oxen is a category of heaven and I was instantly besotted. So much so I became committed to ferrying the divine fuzz to all my friends.

I traipsed about with a plastic bag jam-packed with the stuff. "Stick your hand in." I'd beg, "if I'm right or wrong you'll know it immediately." One and all swooned at the touch. But then what? I had to translate these tufts into practical objects. I've never cared at all about clothes beyond their most basic objective, let alone fashionable clothes. Quite the contrary, I've decried the obsessive nature of trend followers, discounting the mania as silly. I was perfectly content to settle for clean attire and now suddenly I was designing, manufacturing and distributing a high-end line of knitwear worldwide. I remain convinced Alice never peeked through a looking glass quite so cracked as this.

It was spooky to me how easy it was to break into a world that appeared insulated from the outsider. Especially to someone such as me who had such a low opinion of their fascination with the micro-trivia of this year's black. To me, this year's black, was whatever the hell would sell. I'd never previously shopped in the high-end boutiques I would soon be wholesaling to. I'd never bought a copy of *Vogue* in my life, and only ever perused the pages to sop up time in a waiting room. These catalogues that catered to the materialists held zero significance to me.

That is, of course, until my designs began to appear on their pages. Then I bought copies of these magazines and built up an impressive portfolio of screamingly good press.

Another mystification was the unexpected ease behind design. I winced when I thought of the trillions of eager earnest fashion students (and the money their parents bled) diligently studying what turned out to be nothing more than common sense. Clothes, it seemed clear to me, were a highly logical construct. They should fit and flatter the human form. Nothing more and nothing less. Not to say there isn't room for frills and the shock of the new but all I was trying to do was sell sweaters. Due to the magnificence of the raw material the simpler the style the better.

129

To my eternal astonishment my products became a recognizable feature in the rarefied world of fashion.

This should not imply that my interest increased beyond making sales. During meetings with store buyers I'd sometimes nod off as they pored over color charts and made careful predictions of trends massing on the horizon like enemy armies to be conquered. Frequently when asked a question I might have totally lost my train of thought. In the early years I would find a way to cover by aggressively changing the subject. But as time went by and my enthusiasm waned, I'd come right out with the truth and say, "sorry, wasn't listening, what was that again?"

The minutiae of where a button should go, how long a hem might be, the position of a pocket—all of it mattered not a jot to me. As far as I was concerned these stores could order whatever they wanted, any shape, any color. It was all the same to me. I'd say, "Tell me what you want and I'll make it for you."

They knew I was not one of them. I never had the "right" handbag, or "this year's" shoes. But I had the celestial fuzz and they wanted it so they tolerated my failure to fit in. Besides, I couldn't have got it right even if I tried. And on occasion I did try only to fall flat on my unmade-up face. One time, feeling over confident in a very proper dark suit and polished loafers, I happened to start fiddling with my hair, only to discover I had forgotten to brush it. I had a massive dreadlock sticking out like an antennae. Oopsy. There is no fooling that lot. I relied on my product to see me through. I had the crack cocaine of clothing and the customers were addicts.

As the years piled up I learned the ludicrous system of invented seasons and man-made deadlines and gradually lost my life to constant worry and rushing to deliver endless boxes of wool. There were always mistakes and mounting unforeseen stresses, and beneath it all was my greatest foe, that being I had no interest whatsoever in the business. After 8 years I grew tired. Increasingly I was miserable. Worse, I could see no possible exit plan.

Recruiting editorials was the easiest part of the business because journalists need content, and I accumulated reams of good press. Selling to stores was not so awful because these buyers were not spending their own money so they were relaxed placing large orders. The private retail customer, on the other hand, was my ultimate bug-a-boo. Many of them became friends and I appreciated their love of what I knew was a worthy purchase. But some of them drove me batty.

The true nightmare was an event called a "trunk show." I never saw any trunks and I don't know where the name comes from. What I knew, after a couple of these trials, was that the retail customer is a perfectly normal human soon turned tragically insane.

Grown women who had spent a lifetime making decisions crumbled in the face of questions no more complicated than "Would you like to try it on in black or in white?" God forbid they didn't fit into a size medium. You'd think I was a baby killer when I suggested they try on a size large—which I hastily explained was short for "largess," nothing whatsoever to do with "big."

A trunk show meant I would spend a few sweaty hours lugging the merchandize into alluring positions, draping arms and belts just so. Shoppers would arrive, at first perfectly rational beings all of whom would swiftly collapse into what I called the "shopping trance." Quiet as churchgoers their eyes would glaze, their movements slacken, and they'd begin to caress the garments. That's when I knew it was just a matter of time, and I'd have a sale. These shoppers were professionals; in the sense that they shopped regularly. I on the other hand, only sold clothes; I was not and had no claim to be "one of them."

So it was always stupefying when they'd ask me preposterous questions —picking up a cardigan they'd ask me "What do I wear this with?" I could hardly believe they weren't joking. After all, we're talking about a sweater. Frequently caustic remarks came to mind but in view of the opening wallet I'd hold my tongue and give them the ultimate trick answer, "Jeans, that would look great with a pair of jeans." How could they not see right through me, I'd wonder? But they didn't, no in fact they stare at me as if I was the second coming of Christ and say, "I have jeans!" And a sale was made.

Toward the end of those 8 years I began to lose what cool I had and the occasional spiteful comment would shoot forth like an accidentally fired handgun. One woman recklessly complained that my prices were too high, I told her no, and explained the problem was she couldn't afford my prices. I suggested she shop at Kmart, like I do.

While I sold my merchandize for tiny fortunes I personally don't spend much on apparel. I wouldn't dream of paying that kind of money for clothes, really, if I'm going to shell out large sums I want something substantial in return, like a car, not a cardigan.

Another lady told me she loathed her arms, I snapped at her to do some exercise.

And then mercifully the end came. I didn't know it at the time but finally I was hosting my last trunk show. My mood was sour; I was disconsolate but resigned to a life as a handmaiden in fashion hell. I was in the middle of making a sale when a woman I've known for many years sidled up to me. She was blathering on and I was pretty much ignoring her. She was irritating me and unable to control myself I snarled, "Are you here to shop?"

"No," she replied.

"Well then, fuck off," I said, and returned my full attention to my active customer.

"I'm having dinner with Taki and he told me to ask you to join."

Ok, now she had me. Taki Theodoracopulos, author extraordinaire, was not only the inspiration for the central character (the villain) in a novel I'd published 12 years earlier, he was also the love of my life. I met him when I was a teenager and I've never entirely recovered from the experience. For a decade I was spellbound by him. And then one day our union was blown to smithereens by a cataclysmic disagreement.

I had not seen him or spoken to him since. But I'd thought of him often. In a trice I shut down the dreadful trunk show, packed up the woollies and sped off to the appointed restaurant. The instant I saw Taki the gulf of years synched closed. I felt as if I was dreaming and I had no desire to awaken. That same evening he offered me a job writing for his online magazine. In a millisecond I dissolved my wool company and I've never looked back.

Thanks to Taki my life took a magical turn. Once again I had the chance to live life as a writer, and for this I am eternally grateful.

NORML for Aspen

TUESDAY AFTERNOON THE ASPEN, COLORADO Police Department returned a small amount of marijuana to a locally known homeless man. Matthew Franzen, 48, takes the drug to treat glaucoma and he is a state-certified medical marijuana user. Franzen says the police should never have taken his pot from him to begin with. He believes he is being picked on. The police claim they were just following the rules. Possibly, they were goosing the backside of an ongoing grudge.

A recent Saturday Franzen forgot his backpack at the Thrift Shop in downtown Aspen. Store workers found the abandoned bag and delivered it to the police. The police booked the bag, and subsequently discovered the weed within.

According to Franzen the police know perfectly well who he is and what his backpack looks like and all about his status as a legal pot smoker. He says the Aspen police have previously confiscated marijuana from him, only to return it to him after taking their sweet time confirming his name on the state's medical user registry. It was a weekend, then there was a public holiday. They dragged it out, and tortured him. Franzen is certain the police just don't like him.

"They knew I had a certificate months ago," Franzen said. The cops held the drugs in their evidence locker and returned everything else to Franzen. "They took away my pot," Franzen fumed. "That is prescribed medicine for me. They're just harassing me because I'm suing them."

Franzen currently has a civil lawsuit pending against a handful of local law enforcement officials—including the Pitkin County Sheriff's Office and District Attorney's office—for $150,000 in damages. The suit stems from his arrest and imprisonment on burglary charges in November 2007. But that's another story.

Aspen's Police Chief Richard Pryor, a native Brit, conferred with the D.A.'s office on the Colorado medical marijuana statutes before agreeing to release the drugs back to Franzen. Coincidentally, NORML (National Organization for the Reform of Marijuana Laws) is holding a fundraiser in Aspen this weekend for their Hunter S. Thompson Scholarship, which pays for an attorney to attend their annual Aspen Legal Seminar in June.

Creatively maximizing on the circumstances, Lauren Maytin, an Aspen-based criminal defense attorney who is on the Colorado board of NORML, offered to help educate the Aspen Police Department on current medical marijuana law. Franzen has been invited as a guest, Maytin said.

"I'm still a little angry," Franzen said. "But at least I can see again."

She was a Bitch

SHE WAS A BITCH. Men wanted to do her. Women wanted to kill her. She was

the type to tell a man if prostitution was legal she'd gladly ho-out. She'd

piecemeal this morsel during the "job," printing the information into him, like

she was a fax machine. It was rumored she lived with stacks of cash in her

freezer. She was the type to tell a female acquaintance "It's alright for you to take

the subway, but when you look like me you can't."

　　She grew up on the on the shabby side of a chic community. Some

summers she worked as a waitress on a catering detail. The experience drilled her

with envy and craving. Once she saw the inside of mansions, and the glittery

trappings, she made a plan right there and then. Somehow, someday she'd get hers. She had been a fat teenager, but in her 20s, she discovered cocaine and swiftly shed those pounds. Turned out that beneath the behemoth was a goddess. A goddess only minutely marred by a pointy chin. Men responded to her as never before, and as she says, "It was heady." No pun intended I'm sure.

Her 20s and 30s were spent hooking in a super-upscale way. She collected an impressive list of attendant "benefactors." They adored her ease with sex, taking the onus off of them, and for this she was rewarded. But she was a greedy bitch, and the more she saw, the more she wanted. In her late 30s, just as the fantasy was starting to fracture with disillusion, she met an aging French movie star.

As only a true pro could, she had him believing she had no clue who he was. So when she went home with him that night, the very same night they met, he sincerely believed she was smitten with him for him rather than his legend. No one ever had the heart to tell the French movie star he'd hooked up with everyone's favorite hometown ho.

They have been together coming on a decade. He worships her. She has yet to stop grinning. She got her mansion. Apparently she is fond of exclaiming, "I'm a rich person."

Rich bitch.

Super Foot Balls

IF YOU ARE LIKE ME and you don't understand football and you don't care to learn the rules of football, I am delighted to announce I have a solution! You can join the fun without caring a jot or learning a single fact about the game.

Until recently my exposure was limited to walking in on my father transfixed by his TV. Usually I was shushed out of the room. On rare occasions he attempted to enlighten me.

"Keep your eyes on the quarterback!" he'd say.

"Huh?"

"He's the one with the ball." Dad would say. I could never pick out this "quarterback," or the ball. All I saw was opposing line-ups of obese squatting hulks. After a spate of yelling in indecipherable codes the lunks smashed into each other. Except for the rare occasion when a player sprints free for a second or two, only to be leapt upon by a lethal pile of beef-boys.

"Extraordinary athletes," Dad spoke directly to the television imparting advice and suggestions. Until an unfortunate sod made a bad play, and then he would lash admonishments. "Schmuck," he'd mutter.

In later years, to appease boyfriends, I struggled to comprehend the rules. I soon tired of hearing about sacks and carries. I couldn't cotton to the whys behind so many time-outs, and penalties. I could barely suppress laughing at the deadly earnest umpires heavy-breathing into whistles, childishly waving flags, or making crazy arm gestures like traffic cops on crack. I found it massively dull. I gave up and resorted to making plans of my own for Sunday afternoons and Monday nights.

Lucky for me one boyfriend took me to see a real live football game in Gadsden, Alabama and at last I found a way in. Here is some amazing news! Not all football players are enormous screen-filling thugs. Turns out many of them are awesomely sexy. Repeat after me, "objectify and deconstruct," until all you see are the mesmerizingly perfect muscles, as beautiful as any museum quality statuary. Closely observe the graceful kickers with their entire head-to-toe lean toned package. Sorry to be superficial, sexist and demeaning. I'm told these footballers—some of them—have terrific chess brains. They mastermind plays quick as whips to fake out foes. I'm willing to believe this is true, but I really don't give a toss. I am busy admiring the splendor on the Astro-Turf.

Mi Casa Su Hell

IN 2003, THREE AMERICAN MEN, civilian contractors, crashed their plane in the southern highlands of Colombia. They were picked up by FARC guerillas and held prisoner for five and a half years. This spring Morrow publishes their memoirs, *Out of Captivity*. This story was of particular interest to me because some time ago I bought a hill in southern Colombia. My hill was 15 acres with two bamboo forests, a river, and a coffee plantation. The coffee was cultivated by a collective of farmers from the nearby village of San Agustin. Everything imaginable grew on this hill, from eucalyptus trees to banana trees, orange trees, mango trees, and lemon, lime and guanaba trees. Yucca and potatoes and peanuts grew out of the crimson earth. I loved this place on sight and quickly set about building a house with no guest rooms. Because if I was sure of only one thing it was that no guests would ever be visiting.

After a few years the FARC stopped in for a visit. Unfortunately, they did not come with a welcoming casserole. At gunpoint they outlined a three-day evacuation plan with instructions to get home and let "my president" know that they were the "good guys." Gun-toting guerillas aside I have fond memories of my time in Colombia and I was aggrieved to read that what had been my holiday destination was described by the three American civilian contractor hostages as "hell."

At the start of their confinement the Americans were as indignant as they were petrified, and they clung to each other. As months grew to years the bond between them took a bashing. Life in the jungle presented them with unprecedented hardships. No matter how much their private allegiances fluctuated, they remained united against their captors. They never befriended the FARC. All they saw were dangerous terrorists who they despised for their "commie" ideals.

It took a long time for the three Americans to note that these "terrorists" were children, mostly in their teens—simple people who had been promised a bellyful of lies in exchange for their muscle. These people were easily duped because their own lives were horror-shows of backward living with zero possibility of improvement or opportunity.

To the confessional quietude of their notebooks the hostages admitted they'd accepted the high-risk jobs in the Colombian jungle because of fat paychecks. Now they dreamed of freedom and comforts once taken utterly for granted. The FARC is comprised mainly of "campesinos"; country folk born into medieval homesteads hours by foot up narrow mountain paths. Their homes are single-room structures with walls made of mud and straw and cow dung. Earth-dirt floors and a corrugated iron slab for a roof. The "kitchen" is outside—a wood burning oven—and that's it. Livestock roam through scratching at fleas. It is the Middle Ages, rife with rumor and misinformation.

The average campesino believes a blend of truths and home-brewed myths, like all Americans are amoral gangsters. Or that they are bionic super-humans with direct access to heads of government. Some believe Americans are surgically equipped with microchips implanted in their skin and can be tracked down anywhere on the planet. The hostages whined about the bland food, the harsh clothes they were provided, the mud they slipped on and the arduous lifestyle. This incessant complaining was a surprise to the FARC and at odds with their idea of all Americans as bad-ass "Rambos."

Half the time the prisoners feared for their lives, while the rest of the time they debated whether being dead might be better than having to endure the miserable experience.

The FARC think these Americans are pussies. They tramp in these same rubber boots, up and down this muddy landscape every day and wonder when the world will come rescue them from their misery. This is exactly why they are fighting their own oppressors, as they see things.

The FARC ask, "Why are you attacking us?"

The answer is: "We are attacking the drug trade and you are involved."

The FARC say: "We have nothing to do with drugs, we only tax them."

The Americans noted that the Colombians did not indulge in drugs. If anything they were addicted to sugar and would wolf down bricks of "canella". The Americans mistakenly assumed there exists a thread of logic and daily they nag, "What's going on?", "Where are you taking us?" endlessly sifting for information. The answer they get is: "Quién sabe?" There is no plan, nothing beyond evading capture.

The FARC are given orders to keep their wards alive. But most important is not to be caught by the Colombian army. So they move their prisoners constantly.

The FARC don't like "prisoner duty." It's not what they signed up for. They were seduced by the hope of a better life, to be the next Che, and they find themselves running jungle hostels. They wanted dignity and they ended up on a hospitality detail. They say, "We are your hostages because we have to keep you alive."

The Americans are warned not to escape. They are told the Army will kill them and blame it on the guerillas. "To sully our reputation." Meanwhile the FARC is excited with the promise of glory on the horizon. They talk excitedly about how, in order to properly release the three hostages there should be a ceremonial event with ambassadors and bigwigs and the international press.

The Americans take no pity on the bleakness of the lives of these tricked teenagers. But they are not immune to the unusual beauty of their surroundings. After several months their notebooks fill with mentions of views and the multiplicity of flower species. They note the thundering chaos of the tropical rain storms. Come and gone in a matter of minutes. These storms travel fast up a valley, passing overhead and turning the lights off with clouds and crazy water, all soon gone. Afterwards comes a bright sunny sky, with nature dripping dry. One hostage writes of a bug. "It was the most beautiful butterfly I'd ever seen."

On the run from the Colombian army life in the jungle was chock full of absurdities. Centered around tarps, chicken soup and ill-fitting rubber boots, nightly campfires and guitars and songs. The Americans marveled at the skills the FARC have with their machetes. They interpret this level of skill as proof of how long they've been hiding out in the jungle. In reality, the machete is the only tool these campesinos have. They've been using the machete for generations.

When I was building my house I would travel to Colombia with suitcases filled with power tools. I'd spread out the techno wizardry and these skilful artisan workers would look them over. Approvingly checking out each item. Then they'd pick up their machete and a rock and get back to work.

Today the hostages are free and home with their families. The FARC remain in the jungle. Everyone retreated to the comfort of their respective world views. I wonder if anyone is enjoying my house on the hill.

State of the Estate

ROUND ABOUT PRESIDENT'S DAY, every year, the Hamptons summer rentals are locked up tight as a chastity belt. Typically, the best of these resort-centric lush, plush estates, on offer from Memorial Day through Labor Day, are snatched up by New Year. Everything rents. And, ordinarily, for a tidy fortune.

Grimly, there is nothing ordinary these days. You can't rent, sell or give away your blasted property. A formerly unheard-of flood has seeped into an enclave oft considered untouchable.

"The phones are not ringing," a realtor reveals. Agents and homeowners alike expose a shocking new trend. The usually easy-to-move under $100,000 listings are down 80 percent to 90 percent. The high-end market from $100,000 to $1 million has vanished entirely. Think of the summer vacations foregone. Pity the surplus incomes denied. "Buy a house," a neighborhood newspaper touts in a column titled: "Things to do in the Hamptons."

"There are plenty of bargains," a village broker assures, with endearingly faux cheer.

"Ha!" responds a local naysayer, stomping the notion to smithereens. "These same 'experts' who claim that NOW is the time to buy a home on Long Island are morons. Let's see how vocal they are in a few weeks when the towns introduce yet more tax hikes!" Desperate to close a deal an agent recently resorted to negotiating payment of the homeowner's outstanding medical expenses as part of the transaction. Cataclysmic for some, but not for all.

Overheard at a drugstore, a cashier chuckled, "I'm glad to see these dumb bloated prices come down. Now maybe normal people can afford to live around here."

Hellfire and Khakis

NEW YORK—IT IS AFTER MIDNIGHT on a Saturday at Hellfire, a 20-year-old fully equipped S/M fetish dungeon in Manhattan's Meatpacking District. Most of the naked men shuffling about with penis-in-hand are clean-shaven preppies and Wall Streeters. Naked except for an expensive pair of loafers or a button-down shirt, or merely a high-end watch, these are clearly men of substance: decent upstanding citizens with a penchant for deviance. The dread of running into an acquaintance is overcome by the obsessive need behind the deed. Which is maybe why the lights are always low at the Hellfire Club.

"Coming here instead of going home proves these guys are trying to fill an emptiness. They're lonely, they are all missing something in their lives. And

I'm not just talking about underwear." Tony pauses and laughs at his joke. Darkening, he adds, "I'm here, so I must be some kind of freak too."

Tony, a computer analyst at IBM, could not look less like a freak. He is 27, born in Puerto Rico, transplanted to Manhattan 20 years ago. Tony is 6-foot-1, slim, with mocha-colored skin, wavy black hair and a friendly smile. His Docksiders and cotton leisure wear have a yuppie feel.

"She was very mild," says John, discussing the dominatrix who has just finished whipping him. John is a preppie lad of 20 or so. His studded dog collar peeks out from beneath a Brooks Brothers shirt. John continues, "I would never bring a girlfriend here. I come here in between girlfriends, when I've got nothing else to do."

"Ready to play?" says Lenny to a young, fat, bored whore in black pleather rigging. Her flesh seeps out. Lenny is wearing only sneakers. He is tall and pudgy and carrying a yellow and black sports bag on his arm. His glasses fog up repeatedly and he smiles as he wipes the lenses on a napkin.

"What do you want to do?" she replies, already leading him by his sports bag to a private stall in the back room of Hellfire, known as "Heaven." With nothing more than a single chain to close them in she sits on a bench and plays with the gleeful naked man, smacking his behind as she goes. Men instantly surround the stall, dicks in hand, masturbating. "Oooh, aaaah," moans the hooker playfully, and all the men stare on, entranced, while they jerk off.

152

Blocking the view of another booth, and quietly masturbating, is a Hamptons type with checked short-sleeved shirt, khaki shorts and expensive soft leather shoes. He and a group of men are watching the activities of a couple making out in a booth. They are both men, though one is dressed like a hoochie-mama. The man is naked and masturbating his button-mushroom of a penis and with his eyes closed in rapture, he sucks the foot of his companion who idly surveys the cluster of men, all masturbating, watching "her." They are watching and yet also in a trance.

"I love it up the ass," says Fidel, a corporate masseuse by day, and grumpy S M slave by night. He is naked except for a baggy black leather thong, and a chain around his neck held together with a chunky padlock. He has a strap-on contraption in his hands and he is demonstrating how the rubber dildo fits securely with a tug. "I can't exploit the Internet," Fidel laments, "because it would embarrass my family. They hate what I do, but mostly they're worried friends will find out. And I do run into my corporate massage clients all the time. But I love it too much to give it up. I love golden showers. In one dungeon where I work, I'm known as the community toilet."

Fidel stamps around his pen, fondling his collection of whips, dildos, vibrators, handcuffs and assorted medieval paraphernalia -- like a wheel with pointy spikes to roll against flesh. Fidel is bored; he hates working at Hellfire because the patrons tend to be squeamish tourists. "I prefer the real thing, real

153

dungeons with real doms who know what they're doing." Pointing around the dark room, he complains, "I hate this dump, they're all scum, low-lifes. Besides, I hate men, they all suck. I like good submissive women."

With a disgusted grunt Fidel points at a Leslie Nielsen look-alike reclining in a "blow job chair," his pants open, penis exposed. In front of him stands a woman, a 50-ish wiry blond with orange lipstick, sucking on the proffered penis. A circle of men gathers, masturbating to the scene. There is no audible signal but presumably they all climax because the men release flaccid, spent dicks, and the woman is reapplying her lipstick, and the Leslie Nielsen character is zipping his fly. Very matter of factly, he hops down from the oddly shaped chair and hands the woman her pack of cigarettes.

A professional looking lady, about 40, is sitting on a bar stool chatting to some men when she shimmies out of a navy gabardine suit dress, kicks off dark blue pumps and red panties until she is naked. One man stands behind her propping her up, his stomach acting as a headboard, while another man slips in, in front, literally. He lunges and thrusts with no expression on his face, and the usual ring of masturbators collects in a tight throbbing circle. Each man reaches for the woman with his free hand; she is surrounded, and the men switch turns without ever saying a word. A natural pecking order appears as the gangbang finds its rhythm.

An old couple is nearby in a stall, experimenting with dildos and a battery-operated vibrator. The lady is shriveled and covered with warts and she sits with legs apart while her honey rams her with a variety of objects. "It's ticklish," she complains in a slow drawl. She looks bored, and her man looks aggrieved.

At 5 a.m., Fidel carefully packs his toys into a Tommy Hilfiger sports bag and pulls on black jeans, a black polo shirt and black leather loafers. As he walks briskly to his car, a handsome garbage collector hands two big bunches of rhododendrons to a waitress just off her shift from a fashionable restaurant across the street. Fidel revs his 10-year-old BMW, gray with gray interior, and drives home for a change of clothes, and onward to his day job as a masseuse in clean-cut corporate America.

Just as night life is not relegated to nighttime, clean-cut is not necessarily squeaky-clean. Along with the five o'clock shadow comes other werewolf phenomena. Hellfire is only open from 10 p.m. until dawn Thursday through Saturday and it is always filled to the brim, masturbators elbowing one another in the ribs. Manhattan is host to plenty more pleasure dens, all of them bursting with bursting customers.

David, a regular, says: "There are clubs in a few major cities; elsewhere private parties, and associations as well as a frontier-town welcome on the Web." Chicago boasts a Hellfire Club, as does London, fabled home of the original

Hellfire. According to Fidel the slave, "The scene in England is much better than here. More sophisticated, more experimental."

Patty Kaplan, creator of the 10-year-old show "Real Sex" for HBO, says that sex as entertainment is "very here to stay." Kaplan has a new show premiering this month called "G-String Divas." For one full year, video cameras were embedded in the walls of a Philadelphia strip club. The results will be segmented into 13 half-hour episodes.

Kaplan says, "Ever since AIDS, people have needed to find other ways to get off, besides penetration. That is not to say that 'G-String Divas' is a show to whack off to. It's more of an educational-titillating-docu-soap."

With the shedding of values along with newfound freedoms, sex as leisure sport is more commonplace than ever. Everywhere, demand far exceeds supply. As the trend grows, one has to ask: What is next? Gravity-free sex? Penetrating the atmospheric black hole?

George, a husband who patronizes fetish clubs, says, "People assume this is a male trip. That's simply not right. Myths are sprung by women's magazines with stories on how to handle it when your man says he wants to try handcuffs. This is tired and false." His wife says, "Sometimes I go with him. I always know where he is and what he's doing, so why should I worry?"

At Hellfire men pay $30 to enter. Women are welcome free. George says, "Everybody knows women can get sex for free anytime." On certain nights, a man can enter for free if his female companion is willing to shave her beaver, and flash the ticket lady at the front door. Nights when slave auctions are held, men buy women and take them to the Heaven section for fun. "But you can't take your slave home for keeps." George says. "It's just a game."

Part of a normal life routine except it's S/M. Pure entertainment. George says. "The only thing to be afraid of is who you'll see. For example, one's shrink, that would be disturbing." Sex expert psychotherapist H. says, "It would be worse to run into a patient."

H. (who prefers to remain anonymous) says it's "all perfectly normal. People are bored and lonely, and at the same time the thrill threshold is always going up. And rather than spend the evening home alone in tighty-whities, jerking off to the Playboy Channel, it's more exciting to go where the action is. It's stimulation. Meanwhile, I can never get anyone to go swing dancing with me."

He continues: "These men are not perverts, they're just regular guys. Men being men. Men with enough awareness to know what they need."

George. sounding indignant, responds. "The inclination to pathologize this behavior makes me sad. We don't ask shrinks to explain why we're writers. Why should they be expected to be heard from here?"

What to do with an empty evening, a tossup between a dance class or a visit to Hellfire? David says, "I've been going to these places for years, all over the world. What I'm looking for is the potential to 'trip,' to merge with this other way of being. To experience more of myself. More of life. If I get nothing else, at least I'm out of my head for a few hours. Furthermore, after a long hard day I don't want to "swing dance."

Man and Machine

IF YOU OBEY THE SPEED LIMIT it's a six hour drive from the east end of Long Island to Washington DC. I did it in just under ten. If not for GPS, I might still be on the road. Some biological glitch makes me incapable of following commands. Easily distracted I made countless confused u-turns, and left turns in place of right turns (still get those mixed up), and each time, serene GPS uttered: "recalculating route."

After I checked in at the hotel in DC I lugged my overnight bag down the hall and scuttled in to the awaiting elevator. The heavy metallic doors rattled shut. Sagging against one wall, I leaned my elbow into the panel of lighted buttons. Accidently, I pressed B. for basement as well as P. for penthouse. The machine sank downward and then thrust fast upward, like a panther gathering

momentum to pounce. With a sense of relief I let myself in to room 1201.

Giddy with triumph, I hurled myself onto the sofa in the living room, and

grabbed the remote control. The television screen fired up to grey fuzz with a

blue message: "No signal." Minor snag, I acknowledged, but there were other

rooms and more televisions. In the bedroom I turned on the TV only to see the

same alert: "No signal."

"Why?" I whined, drawing it out like a sigh. I phoned Todd at the front

desk, and he cheerily offered to send help. In a jiffy I heard tapping at my front

door. I opened it to find Jacinto, handsome and hot, he was a tonic to behold. He

strode in and confronted the television in the living room with the resoluteness of

a champion tennis player setting up for a serve. He was focused, he cradled the

remote control in both hands, thumbs worked the buttons. His attention was rapt.

We did not speak.

With the luxury of being unobserved I couldn't resist checking out

Jacinto. I rested my eyesight on his scandalous ass and I felt the nag of a smile.

In a flash Jacinto not only had all the televisions on, but tuned to a boisterous ball

game.

Not complaining, BTW, but what is it with men and machines?

Why Pay Less?

LAST NOVEMBER the town of Water Mill saw citizens at war. Camps remain angrily divided into those for and those against the introduction of a Subway sandwich shop in the shopping mall already inhabited by Citarella on Montauk Highway. The divisively emotional issue of national chain stores scuffing up enchanted main streets, pock-marking the prim faux-colonial over-priced shopping havens is one of the touchiest topics on local government rosters. Small business owners and local residents alike crave the preservation of their downtowns and feel it is an uphill struggle to maintain the rural ambiance while also allowing progress to come plunder their quaintness.

McMansion Owner, Water Mill:

> "I don't want a Subway in my town. And I don't want telephone poles. And I don't want anyone building or farming near the Pond. I moved out here 20 years ago and there wasn't nearly as much traffic, and the pond was clean. So I told all my friends to build houses too. Now we have enough houses out here, so no more people can live in Water Mill."

Lowly Underpaid Employee, Water Mill:

> "You obviously forget that not everyone is lucky enough to enjoy your charmed life. But to keep your lifestyle running, you better hope that the less fortunate can continue to survive out here."

McMansion Owner, Water Mill:

> "...and I like paying $9 for a sandwich, so no Subway. Let the local riff raff head west (where I came from 20 years ago) and buy affordable houses and lunch."

Lowly Underpaid Employee, Water Mill:

> "If you want the "riff raff" as you call them to move west, who do you expect will make your 'special sandwich' for you?"

But you have to ask yourself, since it is the Hamptons, why pay less?

Cruise to Nowhere

A FRIENDLY SOUNDING GUY left a message announcing I'd won a free 2-night cruise for me and a companion. I have been known at times to be a bit of a sloth but curiosity is an excellent motivator.

Yes, I phoned. A man named Tom was excited to tell me I was the lucky winner. He shouted the good news into my ear, "You've won a cruise!" I waited for him to regain his composure and began a line of questioning Johnny Cochran would have applauded.

"Who are you guys? Do you have a website? What are the restrictions on this offer? Are you going to ask me for a credit card number?" I inquired. Yes, he'd like my credit card number. Ah ha, my suspicion confirmed. He bristled at my distrust.

"What do you think? I'm gonna take your card number and go to the track, and risk my job?" He asked.

"Have a nice day," I sang at him, and hung up.

Sloth may be sinful but scammers make me seasick.

On Wants

I HAVE LONG ESCHEWED THE MATERIALIST and joshed at the slaves of greed. But I have a watch fetish. I, the otherwise non-materialistic tomboy is felled by a fob. I, who would rather walk bare foot than bother with shoes at all, will salivate at the sight of the right timepiece. It is unseemly. I couldn't explain it if I tried.

One time, strolling London's Portobello Road, my eye settled on a marvel. It caught my fancy, and then as surely, my heart. A face was all there was, a wide circle of orange gold, without so much as a bracelet. So unwanted was this paraplegic the vendor started the price too low to bother arguing. He was

chuffed to be rid of this orphan and he was only a few pennies off paying me to

take it. I took the crippled mechanism to a watch doctor. After some radical

surgeries the beast became a beauty. With a strip of black gros-grain satin for a

band, my watch was magnificent. We lived some splendid years together.

I know precisely the day it vanished. In a messy move from London to

Marrakech, my darling of a watch became lost in space. Life went right on along.

But in a low-grade, invisible way, I became unwell. An unquenchable nausea

invaded at the slightest memory of my lost love. I quietly lived with this

heartache that could make me lose my balance, tip me into an armchair, dribble

tears down my face. My true love, it turned out, was a thing. I mourned it.

Months later, in the souk of Marrakech, buying almonds, I noticed the

milky arm of a foreign lady. At the end of her slender limb, encircled at the wrist

was a black soft cloth watchband. No question it was my watch. My heart raced,

sweat bunched between my breasts. The almond vendor jabbered on. Then, mid-

negotiations, I bolted from the sacks of nuts and slammed into the crowd,

toppling bodies out of my way. As I neared the lady, I slowed my gait to an

unnatural over-excited hopping, tried to catch my breath, and prepared for the

unlikely show-down. Would she resist? Would she flat-out lie?

Fixated by certainty, I knew that whatever the means, the outcome could

only be the watch and I being reunited. Romeo returns!

I pounced. "Where did you get that watch?"

Needless to say, it was not my watch. Just a grotesquely embarrassing moment for me, and no doubt a frightening one for this lady as she tore away from me.

Over the years I've had relationships with many other watches, all types. Though each had its sex appeal, not one of them ever lived up to that first exhilarating liaison. Nevertheless, I learned that to deny oneself is a shallow victory, so just the other day I indulged in a yummy new watch. Its "Return on Investment" will be an exponential pleasure. Can't really do any better than that.

In a season of gift giving I say, "Get yourself something you desire. Feed the beast of your wants."

Happy New Year

A RECENT FORAY TO MANHATTAN confirmed my decision that it is time for a new start. Not sure where I'm going, but the first step is to lighten my overload of possessions. After five days of merriment in the jazzy city that is New York it was time to depart. Lugging 3 tons of luggage I boarded a bus bound for the East End of Long Island. I was returning to my father's empty summer house, where I am currently installed. I vowed as soon as I get home I'll get on with the divesture.

Aboard, I angled my chair and dozed most of the ride. When I awoke I saw undulations of white. Had we somehow slid inside a marshmallow? I thought I had bought a ticket to Southampton, Long Island, but I'm looking out the window and we are deep in arctic tundra.

Miraculously I was delivered to the drop-off spot, right out front of the Southampton train station. The road was obscured by packed snow. White berms swept up and across what looked like a frozen lake, completely filling the public car park. My car was in there, somewhere. Rumor has it on the night of the blizzard plow drivers were sharing beers and a good time, and only one single truck was out working. A "Shout Out" to the Town of Southampton.

I kept the heaviest of my 3 bags beside the road and in platform boots I forged into the polar landscape. At its deepest the snowfall was mid-thigh. With perseverance and sodden socks I reached my car. I was startled to find myself in the throes of such a demanding ordeal.

The engine turned over and then I proceeded to ram back and forth a few feet creating a trench.

Pointless. I employed all my options of 4 wheel drive, low, high, even "tank-extravaganza anti-Armageddon" mode.

Worthless. A taxi company said 30 minutes. No problem. Probably take me that long to retrace my steps to the road. All around was white, the suitcase black. I kept staring at the spot where it had been. T'was gone. My luggage was missing.

Any lasting hint of my glamorous New York City venture was shed. No doubt whoever took my bag was expecting stacks of cash, while t'was nothing other than dirty clothes. I still had the vital items: laptop, wallet, and my shiny new watch. A second "Shout Out" goes to the douche who filched my bag.

The cab dropped me at the end of the unplowed driveway to my dad's house. In ecstasy I confettied the driver with money and clambered home. Once indoors I cranked the heat and abruptly the onerous adventure was behind me. And now a New Year is dawning, it's time to chart a fresh course. I'll be traveling light.

Reluctant Chef

DRAG LAZY SELF from sofa.

Fill a large pot three quarters with water. Place on stove and set to high.

Gather spaghetti, jar of pesto, tub of grated parmesan cheese, plate and fork.

While you wait drop two slices of bread into toaster. When crispy, slather with

butter and drape with slabs of cheese. Eat.

As you finish stuffing your face with the second cheese sandwich the pot

of water should be boiling briskly. Turn stove off, remove pot and dump water in

sink. Return pot (cleaner than before) to cabinet.

Return food stuffs to points of origin, plate and fork on shelf, in drawer.

Wipe crumbs from mouth, and slump sated on sofa.

Sweet Home

I'M MOVING AGAIN. It seems a short while ago I dragged my possessions into this house in Sag Harbor. September 2008. I never unpacked. It is Sunday and I'm faced with Tuesday next, my official move-out date, and I've got nothing lined up. Not that I haven't had the time, just sort of lost track of it. I know I'm moving for sure because I'm just starting to find where things are. Yesterday I figured out how to switch the light on in the kitchen.

Being as it is autumn, there's an abundance of available rentals. Whittling the selection are my criteria: cheap and quiet. I went to see a train carriage, up a dirt path, stuck back behind some other actual houses. I sent a text to the owner to say, no, no way Jose. He promptly strafed me with texted questions. He needed to know right now, exactly, why did I not want his home? He pressed on, urgently, repeatedly, begging for a reason.

I fell instantly in love with a perfect cottage, up wide shale steps, with sky-blue-trimmed welcoming French doors and a cheery capacious interior. The back garden was hemmed by a fern-draped rock wall. An inky dark blue oval swimming pool sparkled center stage. It was all beyond charming. But behind a thin copse was an active lumberyard with trucks the size of trees. Gingerly I trod through an ancient mariner's dwelling where rancid smells lived close to the low ceilings. I tripped over the warped, seasick-inducing plank floors. I had to run outside to gasp air.

One house I walked in to find the realtor had the televisions blaring, alerting me to the probability we were surrounded by noise. I looked back out to the street. Ah, a bus route. A lady moving to Florida was desperate to offload her creepy trailer. The agent described it as "Adirondacks," which turned out to mean fusty and best suited to a goblin.

Jane, with the East Hampton townhouse, arranged for her friend Mike to show me her home. But when I went to get the key he said he'd forgotten it—it was in his other car.

"What are you looking to rent?" Mike posed.

"I need something by Tuesday," I said.

"I have a pool house you can rent. It's just me, and my dog, and 60 acres." Yucko! But thanks anyway. I settled for a Victorian house up a hill, down the street, a few blocks from where I am.

Home at last. Again.

Roger Maris

IF WE HAVE TO GIVE UP water-boarding our enemies I have a terrific suggestion for a replacement torture: off-season in the Hamptons. Bored out of my mind with the windswept eerie nothingness of Sag Harbor village. I tromp around clawing vainly at the shroud of life, looking for fun pursuits.

I overheard (all right, I was actively eavesdropping) a couple of sots chatting about Tom Clavin, and something about him having recently turned in a manuscript

"OMG, I know that name…who is he?" I thought. "Obviously a writer…I love writers." I accosted the louche loudmouths and begged for an introduction. The booze brothers easily upped the necessary information and I was off, sprinting home to send an email request to Clavin and beg for time to interview him. Clavin sounded eager. Too eager, I thought. Something is off. A quick research on the search engines revealed nothing. Stupid search engines, I thought…

So as to best prepare for the encounter I had to ask him what might his book be about? "It's a biography of Roger Maris." Who the friggin heck is Roger Maris? On this topic the search engines spat rapid-fire bulk information. A baseball star from the 50s. Further, Maris is of Croatian descent. I am half Serbian and in the spirit of my feuding ancestors I was already abrim with loathing. It is my ancestral duty to hate the sum-byotch. I care nothing for baseball, or Croats, but I was convinced I'd heard of Thomas J. Clavin so I ignored the fact that Google apparently hadn't and I pushed on with my play-date.

I arrived at the appointed place at the appointed time. Typical loserville Sag Harbor, I was the only customer in the restaurant. I set up my spiral notebook and a couple of pens to affect the look of the seasoned reporter. Clavin sauntered in and, after a howdy-doody with the bartender, who he seemed quite familiar with, and the support of a glass of Chardonnay, and a spare glass filled with ice cubes (which he gradually slipped into the wine before taking sips), I began the quiz.

"Why Maris?"

"…I chose to write about Roger Maris because he was one of our finest athletes, maybe the best, and yet proportionally overlooked. All the better-known players were loved for their antics yet here was a man who had a superb record on the field yet was the least lauded off it. He was a bit of a square…" Feigning fascination in Clavin's every word, I scribbled notes as he spoke, but my tiny mind had wandered off. "…Maris grew up in Minnesota and North Dakota, and he spent his life at odds with his Croatian heritage versus his American citizenship…"

My tummy murmured faintly and I began to daydream of the braised short ribs and mashed potatoes this restaurant is famed for. But I'm a professional and I revealed nothing of my cravings, instead cleverly muttering "ah ha's" at just the right lulls in Clavin's delivery.

And on he went.

"…Maris was the first person to get chewed up by the press on account of his personal life, rather than his playing abilities. The press hated him and went after him. I think it had something to do with his having no charm…" Then I remembered the superb tiramisu I'd once enjoyed for dinner here. No, no, no, I thought, stay away from fattening food.

"Are you against players using steroids?" I asked to clear my head.

"…Mickey Mantle never took steroids and he was the best player ever."

"Yeah well, Mantle is dead." I said, shooting my whole wad of sports trivia knowledge in one blast.

Clavin and the bartender got into a jovial debate on the merits of the signed baseball and the various values of signatures. And just as I debated ordering up a full three-course meal, Clavin said he needed to rush home to his manuscript and the revisions his editors had asked for. Tom's book will be published by Simon & Schuster in the fall.

Later that same evening, back in my rented home, I noticed a business card. I'd seen this card before and paid it little heed. It belonged to the true owner of my temporary domicile. And there it was, in bold it read: Thomas J Clavin, "writer." Finally I realized that's why I recognized Clavin's name; he's a friend of my landlady.

Oh well. It was still way better than an evening alone.

Pat the Hat

IT SEEMS LIKE JUST THE OTHER DAY WHEN MY LATE FRIEND PAT was buried along the rural southern shore of New Jersey. He was dead at 85 from cancer of pretty much everything. His dying wish was to be cremated and placed atop his wife's plot. She died 16 years earlier, and he has missed her each and every day he had to spend without her. Now he will lie above her throughout eternity. Not a bad choice, as choices go.

A Roman Catholic priest officiated in his official white cassock and purple table-runner shawl. He almost looked stylish except he wore an ugly black and white ski jacket over his vestments. "Sorry," he said, sniffling loudly and grabbing for a handkerchief in a pocket of his plastic coat, "I can't take the cold."

He spoke solemnly about preserving the memory of the dead by remembering to speak of them, reminding me of a theme close to the heart of Nikos Kazantzakis of "Zorba the Greek" fame. He might have sounded elegant, too, had he not sped through the eulogy, again, blaming the cold, "sorry, you understand if I wrap this up," he was snorting into his handkerchief. His rushed performance took a somber affair and mangled it into a Monty Python skit. When all was said, he was the first to take his leave, hunch-shouldered and wide steps taking him away. It was cold.

The cemetery was good-looking, a little orchard of death. I couldn't help but think that this business of taking up space in expensive boxes in the earth is a pointless waste of perfectly good real estate. That Pat wanted to be cremated was fine by me. But we mourners shivered and the priest's nose had been an unsettling sight. And Pat was now a mere pile of ash in his urn, straddling his wife's earthen mound.

Humans are essentially protein. And a scientist friend of mine tells me that, incredibly, any protein can be turned into a fiber. And, of course, any fiber can be knitted or woven. Ergo, Pat could be a hat. On that chilly winter morning wouldn't it have been so much kinder to remember dearly departed Pat while wearing him, as a scarf, gloves and a hat, to keep and cherish? Amen.

We Need to Talk

TODAY I GOT A CALL.

"Hi Christina, this is Cindy with FedEx. How is your day going?"

What? Could she really be calling to ask me how my day is going? Then the lady asked, gently, why I wasn't shipping anything these days. She wanted to know if I was doing business with another shipping carrier. I told her I thought she was being a bit nosy. She explained that FedEx was looking closely at all their accounts and was actively seeking ways to improve business. I assured her that I'm not canoodling with the competition. Just so happens I'm not doing much shipping these days.

Next she started begging. It got embarrassing, "FedEx wants to know what we can do better. If you are using another company we want to know what we're doing wrong."

I told the lady to tell her boss not to get his knickers in a twist and that I remain faithful to FedEx. I felt like I was soothing a suspicious lover. Except we're talking about a large corporation, not a lover. Is this a sign of a fracture? I don't know if this qualifies as "insider trading," but if you own Federal Express stocks you might want to sell, sell, sell.

About the Author

Christina Oxenberg was born, and briefly raised, in New York City. This was followed by prolonged stays in London, then Madrid, then back to New York before returning to London, and so on, until after fourteen schools and a multitudinous array of stepparents and their tribes of offspring, a precedent for adventure was set.

Bypassing university, Oxenberg plunged into a whirlpool of random employment, everything from researcher to party organizer to art dealer to burger flipper.

Oxenberg's single true love is writing and she published her first book, TAXI, a collection of anecdotes, in 1986. Despite the lousy pay, Oxenberg published articles in *Allure* Magazine, *The London Sunday Times Magazine*, *Tatler*, Salon.com, *Penthouse* and anyone else who would have her.

In 2000 Oxenberg was seduced by the offer of a regular paycheck and she fell down the rabbit-hole world of fine fibers. In the blink of an eye a decade vanished into an unwieldy wool business. With relief she returns to the relative calm of writing fiction. Between excursions, she lives in New York City.

Copyright ©Leigh Vogel

7341429R0

Made in the USA
Charleston, SC
20 February 2011